JANICE PILSON

Florida Day Trip Adventures

The Spontaneous Person's Guide To A Well-Planned Day Of Fun In Florida

Introduction

I grew up in Sarasota, Florida, in the 1960s, a time when finding a place to be alone wasn't difficult. You could drive along the Gulf with the windows down, the salt air filling your lungs, the sun glinting off the water, and the sound of the waves rising above the steady hum of your engine. Quiet roads led to sleepy fishing villages, untouched beaches, and moss-draped hammocks where time seemed to slow down. Back then, Florida was wild, open, and unspoiled. But today? Today, it's different.

Florida has become a place of towering condominiums, sprawling theme parks, manicured golf courses, and packed beaches. The hidden corners that once made Florida feel like a secret are harder to find. But here's the good news—those places still exist. You just have to know where to look, and that's exactly why I wrote this book.

My name is Janice Pilson, and I'm incredibly excited to be writing this book. Florida is a breathtakingly diverse state, rich with natural beauty and hidden treasures. From the quiet, winding rivers of the Panhandle to the crystal-clear springs of Central Florida, from the wild, tangled mangroves of the Everglades to the forgotten stretches of coastline where time seems to stand still—this is the Florida I want to share with you.

Having lived and traveled all over the state, I've spent years exploring Florida's backroads, springs, and sleepy towns, making it my mission to uncover the places that still feel like the Florida of decades past. This guide is for the local who wants to escape the crowds without traveling far and for the visitor who isn't interested in standing in long lines or paying for another overhyped, overcrowded attraction.

This guidebook is all about stepping away from the crowds and rediscovering the quieter side of Florida—the one that doesn't make it into the glossy brochures. You won't find major theme parks, tourist-packed beaches, or high-rise resorts in these pages. Instead, this book will take you to the places where Florida still feels wild and unspoiled.

Here, you'll find nature-based adventures that don't require months of planning—just simple, beautiful day trips that let you breathe in the fresh air and experience Florida as it once was. Whether it's wading into a crystal-clear spring, meandering down a forgotten coastal road with nothing but pelicans overhead, or exploring a small town where the old Florida charm still lingers, these are the kinds of places you'll discover in this book.

If you're looking for a day spent outdoors, away from the hustle and bustle, you're in the right place.

This book is organized around seven major cities—Pensacola, Tallahassee, Gainesville, Jacksonville, Orlando, Tampa, and Miami—making it easy to plan day trips no matter where you are in the state. Whether you're craving a shaded trail, a quiet fishing dock, or a sandy road that leads to solitude and adventure, you'll find it here. And if you're the kind of traveler who enjoys the journey as much as the destination, take the time to find and follow Florida's scenic byways and backroads—they often lead to the most memorable experiences.

And even with all that's packed into this book, there are still so many more adventures waiting to be discovered. Don't be afraid to follow a signpost for a local park, a roadside farm stand, or a historic site you hadn't heard of. Some of Florida's best treasures aren't marked with fanfare—they're found by wandering with your eyes open and your curiosity intact.

So if you're ready to trade the crowds for something quieter, let's hit the road. The Florida you've been longing for is still out there—wild, peaceful, and full of surprises.

How to Use This Book

The majority of the trips in this book are within approximately a two-hour drive from one of seven major cities—Pensacola, Tallahassee, Gainesville, Jacksonville, Tampa, Orlando, and Miami. The book is organized by city, so all you have to do is find the chapter for the area you're in (or near) and pick a destination that sparks your interest.

I encourage you to ditch the busy highways whenever possible and take the scenic backroads instead. The journey is just as important as the destination, after all. Whether you prefer exploring on foot, by bike, or even by kayak, this book is here to help you craft the perfect Florida day trip—one that takes you away from the crowds and into the heart of the state's natural beauty.

What You'll Find in This Guide

Each destination includes details to help you plan, including:
- **Driving distance** from the nearest major city.
- **Estimated costs** for parking, entrance fees, or rentals (if applicable).

NOTE: Many places offer military/veteran discounts, as well as senior and other. Discounts are not always advertised, so remember to ask!

- **Pet policies**, so you'll know if your furry friend can tag along.
- **Suggested supplies** to help you make the most of your trip.

Tips for the Road

A good day trip is part planning, part spontaneity. Here are a few tips to help you make the most of your adventure:

- **Keep a "picnic pack" handy.** A few utensils, napkins, a small knife, salt and pepper packets, and wet wipes can turn any roadside stop into a perfect picnic. Toss in an old blanket for impromptu meals with a view.
- **Bring snacks and water.** Energy bars, nuts, or cracker packs can save the day when hunger strikes before you make it to a restaurant—or when you stumble upon the perfect quiet spot and don't want to leave.
- **Use a real map.** GPS is great, but a good old-fashioned paper map gives you a bigger picture, helping you spot scenic drives, forests, and wildlife areas you might otherwise miss. The *National Geographic State Recreation Atlas* is a solid choice, but any detailed Florida map will do.
- **Keep a portable charger.** You never know when you'll need extra battery life, and a solar-powered portable charger can be a lifesaver on long hikes/paddles/floats.
- **Zip-lock bags are your best friend.** They can hold snacks, keep your phone dry, or serve as a mini trash bag when you're out exploring.
- **Take your time.** This book isn't about rushing from place to place—it's about slowing down and soaking up the beauty of Florida's hidden corners.

- **Weigh the cost of an Annual Pass.** If you plan to visit many state parks you might want to consider purchasing an Annual Park Pass. There are discounts available, so check out the website
- floridastateparks.org/learn/florida-state-parks-annual-pass

Drive Times

All drive times in this book are based on general estimates from the center of each major city—but of course, your actual time may vary depending on where you're starting and which route you take. And if you're anything like me, you might just take the scenic way on purpose. That's part of the fun.

Destinations are listed from closest to farthest from each city center, with estimated drive times to help you plan. Just remember, the time you'll want to spend once you get there is entirely up to you. I've made a few suggestions, but you may linger longer—or zip through quicker—depending on your pace and interests.

While the listed drive times assume the most direct route, I highly encourage using a paper map to find alternate roads and scenic byways. Sometimes the detour leads to a peaceful birding trail, a charming small town, or just a quieter, more beautiful stretch of road.

So grab your map, pack a snack, and let's explore some of Florida's best off-the-beaten-path destinations. The road is calling—and adventure is just around the bend.

Pet Policies

Each location in this book includes information on whether dogs are allowed. While many parks and outdoor areas welcome pets, there are important restrictions to keep in mind.

In general, dogs are not permitted inside buildings, food service areas, playgrounds, restrooms, swimming areas, or on beaches unless specifically designated as dog-friendly. When allowed, dogs must be kept on a leash at all times, except in designated off-leash areas such as dog parks. As a responsible pet owner, always clean up after your dog and dispose of waste properly.

Florida's climate and environment can pose unique challenges for pets. Sand and pavement can become dangerously hot, especially during the summer months, which can burn your dog's paws. Additionally, alligators pose a serious threat to pets. Never allow your dog near freshwater lakes, ponds, or marshes, as alligators see them as easy prey. Be especially cautious during mating and nesting season (April–September) when alligators are more aggressive. Alligators are most active during feeding times—early morning and late evening—so extra vigilance is necessary if you're out near water at those times.

By following these guidelines, you and your four-legged friend can safely enjoy Florida's natural beauty while respecting wildlife and park regulations.

Pensacola Adventures

Nestled along the emerald waters of the Gulf of Mexico, Pensacola is a city where history, culture, and outdoor adventure come together in perfect harmony. Known for its sugar-white beaches, deep naval history, and lively downtown, Pensacola is more than just a coastal getaway—it's a launchpad for some of the best outdoor experiences in Florida.

For those who love the salt air and ocean breeze, Pensacola offers unspoiled beaches, hidden coastal gems, and stunning wildlife preserves. Just a short drive from downtown, you'll find yourself exploring the protected shores of Gulf Islands National Seashore, paddling through the tranquil waters of Big Lagoon State Park, or setting sail from Pensacola Bay on a dolphin-watching cruise. Those looking for an off-the-beaten-path beach day can escape to Navarre Beach or Johnson Beach, where the sand is soft, the water is clear, and the crowds are few.

If your sense of adventure takes you beyond the shoreline, the surrounding region is filled with forests, rivers, and scenic trails. Less than an hour from Pensacola, Blackwater River State Park offers some of Florida's most pristine kayaking and tubing waters, where the gentle current carries you through towering longleaf pine forests. The Juniper Creek Trail and Coldwater Creek provide a peaceful retreat for paddlers and hikers alike, while Tarkiln Bayou Preserve and Blackwater River State Forest invite visitors to explore rare plant species, winding boardwalks, and miles of shaded trails.

Pensacola is also a hub for wildlife lovers and sportsmen. Whether it's deep-sea fishing in the Gulf, birdwatching in coastal marshes, or spotting dolphins in Pensacola Bay, there's no shortage of opportunities to connect with nature. And for those who prefer history mixed with adventure, a visit to Fort Pickens offers the chance to hike among historic ruins, bike through the national seashore, or sit under the stars on a quiet stretch of coastline.

Within an hour and a half of downtown Pensacola, outdoor enthusiasts can find hidden springs, lush forests, peaceful waterways, and some of the most scenic beaches in the country. Whether you're setting out on a kayak expedition, cycling along a coastal trail, or simply soaking up the sun on a quiet shore, Pensacola is the perfect base for your next outdoor adventure.

Pensacola, Florida

Total day trip time: approximately 5 hours. 40-minute drive round trip, leaving 4 ¼ hours for adventure.
Dogs: Check with the company—most do allow.
- **Fees:** Check prices online with the company you select.
- **Activities:** Cruise, beach

Breathtaking Views, Gentle Waves, and Wild Dolphins Up Close!

Exploring Pensacola's waterways by boat is one of the best ways to experience the beauty of the Gulf Coast. Whether you're hoping to spot playful dolphins, take in a breathtaking sunset over the bay, or simply relax on the water, a dolphin and scenic bay cruise is an unforgettable way to see this coastal paradise from a new perspective.

Pensacola Bay is home to a thriving population of bottlenose dolphins, and taking a guided dolphin-watching cruise offers the perfect chance to see these incredible marine mammals in their natural habitat. Dolphins are known for their playful nature, often seen leaping through the waves, riding boat wakes, or curiously approaching passing vessels. These cruises typically explore Pensacola Bay, Santa Rosa Sound, and the Gulf of Mexico, where dolphins are frequently spotted year-round.

On a typical dolphin cruise, passengers can expect up-close dolphin sightings in their natural environment, expert narration from local guides who share insights on dolphin behavior and marine life, scenic views of Pensacola's waterfront, including historic sites and natural landmarks, and a chance to see sea turtles, stingrays, pelicans, and other coastal wildlife

Most dolphin tours last 1.5 to 2 hours and depart from Pensacola Beach, Perdido Key, or downtown Pensacola. Sunset dolphin cruises add an extra layer of magic, with vibrant skies reflecting on the bay as dolphins swim nearby.

For those looking for a more relaxed, sightseeing experience, scenic bay cruises showcase the stunning beauty of Pensacola's waterways, islands, and harbors. These tours often include sweeping views of Pensacola Bay, Santa Rosa Sound, and Big Lagoon, and historic landmarks, including Fort Pickens, the Pensacola Lighthouse, and the Naval Air Station

Sunset cruises are particularly popular, as the sky turns brilliant shades of orange, pink, and purple over the calm bay waters. Some tours even offer specialty options, such as wine and cheese cruises, eco-tours, and fireworks-viewing cruises on holiday weekends.

For a truly unique experience, some Pensacola boat tours offer Blue Angels practice cruises *(Seasonal - March through November)*, allowing guests to watch the legendary U.S. Navy flight demonstration squadron perform aerial stunts from the water. These tours provide front-row views of the Blue Angels soaring over Pensacola Bay, making for an unforgettable combination of history, aviation, and natural beauty.

Whether you're a nature lover, photography enthusiast, or simply looking for a peaceful escape, dolphin and scenic bay cruises in Pensacola offer a chance to experience the best of Florida's Gulf Coast. With pristine waters, abundant wildlife, and unforgettable sunsets, these cruises provide a laid-back, yet exciting way to explore one of Florida's most beautiful coastal regions.

Company	QR	Website	Price range
Jolly Sailing		jollysailing.com/	From $35 to $75
Chase-N-Fins		chase-n-fins.com/	From Adult $30/Child 0-4 $15 to Adult $45/0-4 $25
Premier Dolphin Cruise		pensacoladolphincruise.com	From Adult (ages 13+): $35/Child (ages 0-12): $25 to Adult $50/Child $40
Frisky Mermaid (Also rents pontoon boats)		friskyboattours.com	From $27 to $45
Laguna's		lagunaspensacolabeach.com/dolphin-cruise	From Adult $35/Child $25 to $40+

Suggested Supplies

Water (no glass)	Snacks	Sunscreen
Sunglasses (polarized are best)	Binoculars	Rubber-soled shoes

Pensacola, Florida

Total day trip time: approximately 5 hours. 1 hour drive round trip, leaving 4 hours for fun and exploring.

Dogs: Yes

- **Fees:**
  - $3.00 per vehicle
  - $2.00 pedestrians, bicyclists, extra passengers
- **Activities:** hiking, birding, fishing, wildlife viewing, nature trail

Walk Among Carnivorous Plants and Untouched Wetlands

Spanning over 4,000 acres, Tarkiln Bayou Preserve State Park is a hidden gem along Florida's Gulf Coast, offering visitors a chance to explore a rare and fragile ecosystem found only in this part of the world. This pristine wet prairie habitat is home to an incredible variety of endangered and rare plant species, including four types of pitcher plants, carnivorous plants that rely on insects for nutrients.

One of the park's most fascinating residents is the white-topped pitcher plant, a species that exists only along the Gulf Coast between the Apalachicola and Mississippi rivers. In addition to this unique flora, the preserve protects nearly 100 other rare plants and animals, including the sweet pitcher plant, Chapman's butterwort, and the elusive alligator snapping turtle.

A scenic boardwalk leads visitors through the preserve, offering beautiful views of Tarkiln Bayou and the chance to observe wildlife, native plants, and the untouched coastal landscape. Beyond the boardwalk, the park features hiking trails where visitors can explore deeper into the wetlands, pine forests, and prairie, providing even more opportunities for nature observation and photography.

After a leisurely hike, visitors can unwind at the picnic areas, making it easy to enjoy a peaceful meal surrounded by the sights and sounds of Florida's untouched wilderness. Whether you're a botany enthusiast, a wildlife lover, or simply looking for a quiet place to reconnect with nature, Tarkiln Bayou Preserve offers a glimpse into one of Florida's most unique and ecologically significant landscapes.

Hours	8 a.m. until sunset, 365 days a year
Phone	850-492-1595
Location	2401 Bauer Road Pensacola FL 32507
Website	floridastateparks.org/parks-and-trails/tarkiln-bayou-preserve-state-park

Suggested Supplies

Sunscreen	Water	Snacks
Bug repellant	Waste clean-up bags for Fido	Picnic supplies

Pensacola, Florida

Total day trip time: approximately 4 hours. 1-hour round-trip drive, leaving 3 hours for fun and exploring.

Dogs: Yes

- **Fees:**
  - $6.00 per vehicle (two to eight people).
  - $4.00 single-occupant vehicle.
  - $2.00 pedestrians, bicyclists, extra passengers, passengers in vehicle with holder of Annual Individual Entrance Pass.
- **Activities:** Hiking, swimming, fishing, birdwatching, wildlife viewing

Sunsets, Salt Marshes, and Scenic Trails

Nestled along the shimmering waters of Big Lagoon, this 705-acre state park is a gateway to Florida's pristine coastal beauty, offering visitors a chance to experience tranquil marshes, sandy shorelines, and winding nature trails just a short drive from Pensacola. Whether you prefer to paddle through calm waters, watch for rare birds, or simply enjoy a peaceful picnic by the bay, Big Lagoon State Park is the perfect retreat for those looking to reconnect with nature.

Big Lagoon's shallow estuaries and tidal marshes provide the perfect setting for a peaceful paddle by kayak, canoe, or paddleboard. The park's boat ramps make it easy to launch into the protected waters, where visitors can glide past hidden inlets, saltwater flats, and winding shorelines. Along the way, it's common to see herons wading through the shallows, fish darting beneath the surface, and even the occasional dolphin passing through the lagoon.

Big Lagoon State Park is a stop on the Great Florida Birding and Wildlife Trail, drawing birdwatchers from across the region. Its diverse habitats—ranging from saltwater marshes to pine flatwoods—make it a prime location for spotting migratory birds during the spring and fall months. More than 23 species of wood-warblers pass through the park, alongside sandpipers, black-bellied plovers, and various species of coastal ducks.

Visitors can borrow binoculars from the ranger station and wander through the expansive coastal forest, searching for flashes of color in the trees or wading birds along the shore. For a breathtaking perspective, the three-story observation tower offers panoramic views of the lagoon, marshlands, and even glimpses of the distant Gulf of Mexico.

Big Lagoon State Park is also a hiker's retreat, featuring boardwalks and scenic trails that wind through coastal landscapes, towering pines, and sandy dunes. The East Beach Picnic Area offers easy access to boardwalks that lead directly to the observation tower, while longer trails invite visitors to explore deeper into the park's unique ecosystems.

For those looking to slow down and take in the scenery, the park provides beach wheelchairs free of charge, allowing everyone to enjoy the boardwalks and shoreline views with ease.

After a morning of paddling, birdwatching, or hiking, visitors can unwind at one of the park's many picnic areas, where tables and grills provide the perfect setting for a peaceful lunch with a view. The combination of shaded pavilions, open green spaces, and gentle sea breezes makes Big Lagoon an ideal spot to spend the afternoon soaking in the natural beauty.

Hours	8 a.m. Central time until sunset daily
Phone	850-492-1595
Location	12301 Gulf Beach Highway Pensacola FL 32507
Website	floridastateparks.org/BigLagoon

Suggested Supplies

Water	Snacks	Bug repellant
Waste clean-up bags for Fido bag for Fido	Sunscreen	Picnic supplies
Swim suits	Towels	Blanket/chairs
Water shoes	Binoculars (Available to borrow from ranger station—first come, first served)	

Milton, Florida

Total day trip time: approximately 4 hours. 1-hour round-trip drive, leaving 3 hours for fun and exploring.

Dogs: Yes (Not allowed in visitor center and museum)

- **Fees:**
  - $6.00 Adults
  - $3.00 Children (3 and over)
  - $5.00 Seniors, active military and dependents, AAA, Museum of Art members, and UWF alumni
  - $0 EBT card holders (up to 4 per card)
  - $3.00 UWF students with Nautilus card
- **Activities:** Interpretive history, interactive exhibits, walking, hands-on children's exhibits, interpretive archaeological site

A Journey Through Florida's Industrial Past

Tucked away in the heart of Milton, Florida, Arcadia Mill Archaeological Site offers a fascinating glimpse into the 19th-century industrial boom of Northwest Florida. Once home to a water-powered sawmill, textile mill, and a thriving community, the site now serves as both a historical landmark and a nature retreat, where visitors can explore archaeological remains, interactive exhibits, and scenic boardwalk trails.

The Arcadia Mill Visitor Center is the perfect place to start your journey. Located at the top of the first gravel driveway, this wheelchair-accessible facility features paved designated parking and an entrance ramp for easy access. Inside, the 1,000-square-foot museum exhibit brings Arcadia's rich history to life, highlighting both historical and archaeological discoveries from the site. A special children's area, "Meet Me at the Mill," offers hands-on exhibits, allowing younger visitors to engage with history in a fun and interactive way.

Before heading out to explore the site, be sure to visit the museum store, where you'll find a selection of books and unique gifts related to local history and culture.

Arcadia Mill isn't just about history—it's also a beautiful place to enjoy the outdoors. The elevated boardwalk and bridge, spanning three-fourths of a mile, take visitors through the archaeological remains of the old mill facilities, complete with interpretive signage explaining the historical significance of each feature. This scenic route is wheelchair accessible, ensuring that all visitors can experience the park's natural beauty and historical intrigue.

For those looking to explore further, the nature trails extend beyond the boardwalk, covering approximately one mile of the site. Maps are available at the Visitor Center, helping hikers navigate the short loops to the east and west, where they can experience Florida's lush woodlands and natural landscapes.

Visitors interested in a more immersive experience can stop by the Treetop Classroom, which hosts traveling exhibits, lectures, and educational programming. This space serves as an interactive learning station, making it a popular spot for field trips and special events.

Near the Visitor Center, the Discovery Pavilion offers a unique look at 19th-century technology, featuring working replicas of water-powered mill equipment. Visitors can also engage with an interpretive, six-button sound post, which brings the history of Arcadia to life through audio storytelling.

Arcadia Mill provides plenty of opportunities to slow down and enjoy the natural setting. A shaded picnic area with eight tables offers a perfect spot for families and groups to relax after a walk through the site.

Hours	**Site grounds** including the boardwalk and pavilion at Arcadia Mill Archaeological Site: open year-round, from sunrise to sunset. Arcadia Mill **Visitor Center and Arcadia Homestead** site: Friday and Saturday from 10 a.m. to 4 p.m.
Phone	850-595-5985
Location	5709 Mill Pond Lane Milton, FL 32583
Website	historicpensacola.org/explore-arcadia-mill/hours-tickets/arcadia-mill-archaeological-site/

Suggested Supplies

Water	Snacks	Sunscreen
Bug repellant	Waste clean-up bags for Fido	Stroller or wagon for small children
Picnic supplies		

Gulf Breeze, Florida

Total day trip time: approximately5 hours. 1-hour round-trip drive, leaving 4 hours for fun and exploring.
Dogs: No
- **Fees:**
  - $27.95 Adult
  - $20.95 Child

Each additional attraction is an additional fee. Additional fees range from $35.00 to $50.00. Military discounts available.)
- **Activities**: Wildlife viewing, petting zoo, mining for gems, safari train ride.

Roam with Rhinos, Feed Giraffes, and Explore the Wild

At Gulf Breeze Zoo, wildlife isn't just something you observe—it's something you experience. Whether it's the tickle of a giraffe's tongue, the powerful snap of an alligator's jaw, or the thrill of a safari ride past free-roaming animals, this one-of-a-kind destination brings you closer to nature in ways you never imagined. From hands-on feedings to behind-the-scenes encounters, every visit is an adventure waiting to happen.

For many, the highlight of a trip to Gulf Breeze Zoo is feeding the giraffes. As you hold out a leafy green, you'll feel their long, prehensile tongues curl around the treat, pulling it from your hand in a way that's both graceful and amusing. Those wanting an even closer experience can opt for the Giraffe Encounter, a behind-the-scenes tour of the giraffe house. Here, visitors learn what it takes to care for and protect these towering animals, gaining an appreciation for one of Africa's most iconic species.

A Meeting with a Modern-Day Tank

For those who prefer ground-shaking encounters, the Indian Rhino Experience offers an up-close introduction to Soman, a rare Greater One-Horned Rhino. Standing mere feet away, you'll have the chance to admire his armor-plated skin, learn how he's cared for, and gain a new understanding of these prehistoric-looking herbivores.

Holding a Living Legend

Few creatures inspire as much awe as the American alligator, but at Gulf Breeze Zoo, visitors can go a step further and meet a true rarity— the albino alligator. With their pale skin and piercing eyes, these ghostly reptiles are unlike anything you've seen before. As part of the Albino Alligator Encounter, guests have the once-in-a-lifetime opportunity to hold one of these rare creatures, while learning how their lack of pigment makes survival in the wild almost impossible.

A Sky Full of Color

Inside the Budgie Aviary, a flutter of wings signals the arrival of dozens of tiny, colorful birds. Holding out a treat, you'll soon find yourself surrounded by vibrant parakeets, also known as budgerigars, who eagerly perch on your hand to enjoy a snack. This interactive experience brings the joy of birdwatching to a whole new level, allowing visitors to engage with these gentle, social birds in a way that feels straight out of a storybook.

All Aboard for a Safari Adventure

One of the best ways to explore the zoo is aboard the Safari Line Express, a 15-minute narrated train ride that winds through the zoo's 30-acre preserve. From your seat, you'll spot rhinoceroses, antelope, and deer roaming freely, just as they would in the wild. The ride also offers unbeatable views of gorillas, orangutans, and Nile hippos, giving visitors the chance to see majestic wildlife up close in a naturalistic setting.

Feed the Herd (and More!)

Animal lovers looking for more hands-on experiences will find plenty of opportunities to interact with the zoo's diverse residents:

> Scottish Highland Cows – With their shaggy red coats and gentle nature, these ancient cattle breeds are eager to eat straight from your hand.

> Dromedary Camels – With their thick lips and towering stature, these desert dwellers will happily munch on hay and treats offered by guests.

> American Alligators – From April to October, visitors can watch (or participate in) alligator feeding, witnessing firsthand the power of one of North America's largest reptiles.

Unearth Hidden Treasures

For a different kind of adventure, visitors can try their luck at the Mining Sluice, where they can sift through sand and water to uncover real gemstones, fossils, and arrowheads. Some of these artifacts are similar to what might be found locally, while others come from far-flung corners of the world, making each discovery a little piece of history in your hands.

A Farmyard Full of Fun

No trip to Gulf Breeze Zoo is complete without a stop at The Farm, where guests of all ages can feed and pet friendly barnyard animals, including goats, sheep, and other adorable farm favorites.

An Adventure for Every Explorer

Whether you're seeking thrills, discovery, or a quiet moment observing the wonders of nature, Gulf Breeze Zoo offers a unique, immersive experience that brings you closer to wildlife than ever before. From feeding a giraffe to watching rhinos roam, from holding an albino alligator to riding through a safari landscape, each visit is filled with incredible memories waiting to be made.

For those looking to step into the wild and embrace adventure, Gulf Breeze Zoo is the perfect place to see, touch, and experience nature like never before.

Hours	8 a.m. to 5 p.m. daily
Phone	866-620-1825
Location	5701 Gulf Breeze Parkway, Gulf Breeze, FL 32563
Website	gbzoo.com

Suggested Supplies

(No outside food or drinks allowed)	Sunscreen	Play/casual clothes
Sunglasses	Hat	Binoculars
Stroller or wagon for kids (rentals available)		

Elberta, Alabama

Total day trip time: approximately 4 hours. 1 ¼ hours' drive round trip, leaving 3 ¾ hours for the ride of a lifetime.
Dogs: No
- **Fees:** $279.00 to $500.00 depending on the package you select
- **Activities:** Skydiving

The Ultimate High-Flying Adventure

For a bucket-list worthy, heart-pounding experience, Skydive the Gulf offers breathtaking coastal skydiving unlike anything else along the Emerald Coast. Imagine stepping out of an aircraft 10,500 feet above the Gulf of Mexico, the salty breeze rushing past you as you freefall at 120 mph, the world below an endless expanse of sparkling blue waters, sugar-white beaches, and winding coastal bays.

This is not your typical adventure—this is a thrill-seeker's dream.

From the moment you board the Cessna 182 aircraft, the adrenaline builds. As the plane climbs higher and higher, the view transforms into something straight out of a postcard—Perdido Bay, Orange Beach, and the stunning Gulf Coast shoreline spread out beneath you.

And then, the door opens.

Strapped securely to an experienced instructor, you edge toward the opening, take a deep breath, and jump into the open sky. The rush of pure, unfiltered adrenaline lasts for nearly a full minute of freefall, an intense moment of absolute exhilaration where gravity fades and the world becomes a blur of speed and wind.

At 5,000 feet, the parachute deploys, and the chaos of freefall melts into peaceful serenity. Suspended in midair, you glide gently toward the ground, with unobstructed views of the shimmering Gulf waters and the untouched coastline below. For five to seven minutes, it's just you, the sky, and the endless horizon.

A Sunset Like No Other

For those looking to make this adventure even more extraordinary, the Sunset Beach Skydive takes it to the next level. As the sun dips below the horizon, painting the sky in hues of fiery orange and deep purple, you'll descend into the fading daylight for a one-of-a-kind twilight landing on the beach—a moment that feels more like a dream than reality.

NOTE: must be at least 19 years old and weigh 250 lbs or less

Hours	Monday/Tuesday/Wednesday (office hours only): 8:00 am – 6:30 pm Thursday-Sunday: 8:00 am – Sunset
Phone	850-543-8756
Location	28502 Frank Road Elberta, AL 36530
Website	skydivethegulf.com/

Water	Snacks	

Suggestions and Requirements

- **Dress for comfort and movement.** Wear **close-fitting, weather-appropriate clothing** that won't flap in the wind.
- **Choose athletic shoes**—flip-flops, sandals, and boots with hooks are a no-go.
- **Temperatures at 10,500 feet can be up to 30° cooler than on the ground**, so dressing in **layers** is key. You'll stay warm during the climb and cool once you land.
- **Long hair should be pulled back securely**—your instructor will thank you!
- **Remove any jewelry** before your jump to prevent loss.
- If you wear **glasses or contacts**, don't worry—you **won't have to sacrifice clear vision for the experience**. We'll provide you with **disinfected goggles** to keep your eyewear safe and secure while you soar.
- **Eat a normal meal** before your jump—going in on an empty stomach **can leave you lightheaded**, while overloading on food **can make you feel sluggish or nauseous**.
- **Stay hydrated**, but skip the energy drinks or anything overly sugary before your jump.
- **Avoid alcohol and recreational drugs beforehand**—you'll want to be alert, clear-headed, and ready to enjoy every second of this incredible experience.

Milton, Florida

Total day trip time: approximately 6 hours.1 ¼ hour drive round trip, leaving 4 ½+ hours for fun and exploring.

Dogs: Yes (Not allowed on beaches or in the water)

- **Fees:**
  - $4.00 per vehicle (up to eight people).
  - $2.00 for active Florida National Guard members, holders of an active Florida EBT card, pedestrians, bicyclists, extra passengers, passengers in vehicle with holder of Annual Individual Entrance Pass.
- **Activities:** Hiking, bicycling, swimming, boating, tubing, fishing, wildlife viewing, birdwatching

Paddle, Play, and Explore Florida's Most Scenic River

Tucked away in the northwestern corner of Florida, Blackwater River is a tranquil escape into nature, offering some of the clearest, slow-moving waters in the state. Known for its sand-bottom river, longleaf pine forests, and abundant wildlife, this park is a haven for paddlers, hikers, and outdoor lovers looking to experience Florida's natural beauty away from the crowds.

At the heart of the park is the Blackwater River, one of the purest sand-bottom rivers in the country. The river's gentle current makes it perfect for canoeing, kayaking, or tubing, allowing visitors to float effortlessly past towering pine trees, white-sand banks, and winding forested shorelines. Along the way, it's common to spot great blue herons, turtles sunning themselves on logs, and even an occasional river otter slipping through the water. The soft, sandy beaches along the river provide ideal spots for swimming, picnicking, or simply relaxing in the sun.

For those who prefer to stay on land, Blackwater River State Park offers scenic trails that weave through rolling sandhills, floodplain swamps, and towering pine forests. The Chain of Lakes Trail provides a short but stunning journey along a series of picturesque oxbow lakes and river overlooks, while the Juniper Creek Trail offers a longer, more immersive trek through shaded woodlands, red clay bluffs, and wildflower-filled meadows. Birdwatchers will find plenty to enjoy, with sightings of red-headed woodpeckers, hawks, and migratory songbirds throughout the year.

Beyond its serene landscapes and quiet waters, Blackwater River State Park is a place where time slows down, allowing visitors to reconnect with nature. Whether you're paddling through the gentle currents, taking in the sights along a forested trail, or dipping your feet in the cool, clear water, this park offers an authentic Old Florida experience—untouched, unspoiled, and unforgettable.

Hours	8 a.m. until sundown and the ranger station is open 3 to 5 p.m., 365 days a year.
Phone	850-983-5363
Location	7720 Deaton Bridge Road Milton FL 32564
Website	floridastateparks.org/parks-and-trails/blackwater-river-state-park

Suggested Supplies

Sunscreen	Bug repellant	Water
Snacks	Tubes/floats (For canoe, kayak or tube rentals, please contact Blackwater Canoe Rental at 850-623-0235)	Towels/change of clothes
Water shoes or old sneakers (For floating/boating)	Hiking boots or good walking shoes	Waste clean-up bags for Fido

Pensacola, Florida, is renowned for its stunning white-sand beaches and emerald-green waters, offering both locals and visitors a variety of coastal experiences.

Top beaches in the Pensacola area

Casino Beach

Located at the heart of Pensacola Beach, Casino Beach is the most popular and accessible beach in the area. It features the iconic Pensacola Beach Gulf Pier, which extends 1,471 feet into the Gulf of Mexico, making it one of the longest piers on the Gulf Coast. The beach is equipped with lifeguard stations, volleyball courts, and a variety of nearby restaurants and entertainment options, making it ideal for families and groups seeking a lively atmosphere.

Perdido Key State Park

Situated on a barrier island southwest of Pensacola, Perdido Key State Park offers a more secluded beach experience. The park's pristine white-sand beaches and rolling dunes covered with sea oats provide a tranquil setting for swimming, sunbathing, and surf fishing. Boardwalks from the parking areas lead visitors over the dunes to the beach, protecting the fragile ecosystem.

Johnson Beach at Gulf Islands National Seashore

Part of the Gulf Islands National Seashore, Johnson Beach offers a serene environment with ample opportunities for swimming, birdwatching, and hiking. The area includes a half-mile, self-guided nature trail that winds through a salt marsh and maritime forest, providing a glimpse into the region's diverse ecosystems. Facilities such as picnic shelters, restrooms, and showers are available, making it a convenient spot for a day trip.

Quietwater Beach

Located on the Santa Rosa Sound side of Pensacola Beach, Quietwater Beach lives up to its name with calm, shallow waters perfect for families with young children. The nearby Quietwater Beach Boardwalk offers shopping, dining, and live entertainment, providing a well-rounded beach experience.

Fort Pickens Beach

Adjacent to the historic Fort Pickens on the western end of Santa Rosa Island, this beach combines history with natural beauty. Visitors can explore the well-preserved fortifications dating back to the 19th century and enjoy the unspoiled beaches that are part of the Gulf Islands National Seashore.

Best Dog-Friendly Beaches in Pensacola

For those looking to enjoy the beach with their canine companions, Pensacola offers designated dog-friendly beach areas. These areas provide a safe and enjoyable environment for both dogs and their owners, with amenities such as waste disposal stations and freshwater access. It's important to note that dogs are only permitted in these designated areas and must be kept on a leash at all times. Owners are also responsible for cleaning up after their pets to ensure the beaches remain clean and enjoyable for all visitors.

Pensacola Beach East Dog Park

Located at Parking Lot 28.5, the first parking lot past Portofino, this dog-friendly area also mandates leashes for all dogs. Amenities include doggie bags, disposable bins, and handy wipes.

Pensacola Beach West Dog Park

Situated at the first parking lot past the last condos on the Gulf, at beach walkover 21.5, this designated dog beach requires dogs to be on a leash at all times. Similar amenities such as doggie bags, disposable bins, and handy wipes are available.

Bayview Dog Park and Beach

Located at 2000 E Lloyd St., Pensacola, this park offers an acre of off-leash space overlooking Bayou Texar. Dogs can enjoy both land and water activities in an enclosed area, with wash stations available for post-play cleanup.

General Guidelines for Dog Beaches in Pensacola:

- Designated Areas: Dogs are only permitted at specified dog beaches, such as those at lots 21E and 28B. All other public beach areas and parks on Pensacola Beach are off-limits to dogs.
- Leash Requirements: Dogs must be on a leash at all times while on the beach.
- Operating Hours: Dog beaches are open from sunrise to sunset daily, except during turtle season (May 1 – October 31), when they are open from 7 a.m. to sunset.
- Cleanliness: Owners are responsible for picking up and properly disposing of their dog's waste.

Whether you're seeking a bustling beach with ample amenities or a quiet stretch of sand to relax, Pensacola's diverse beaches cater to a wide range of preferences, ensuring a memorable coastal experience for all visitors.

Please note that while the information provided is accurate to the best of our knowledge, it's always a good idea to check the latest local guidelines and beach regulations before planning your visit.

Tallahassee Adventures

The Tallahassee region of Florida is one of the state's most unique and underrated areas. While much of Florida is known for its tropical beaches, bustling theme parks, and endless tourist attractions, this part of the state offers a different kind of beauty—one that is wilder, more rugged, and deeply tied to history and nature. Here, rolling hills, ancient forests, winding rivers, and hidden springs invite exploration, offering a glimpse into the Florida of decades past.

Unlike the more developed landscapes of Central and South Florida, the Tallahassee area retains a sense of Old Florida charm. The city itself feels more Southern than tropical, with its grand oak-lined roads, historic plantations, and quiet, scenic byways. The region has deep Native American roots, with sites like Lake Jackson Mounds State Park offering a window into the civilizations that thrived here long before European settlers arrived. The area is also rich in Florida's colonial and early statehood history, making it a fascinating destination for those who enjoy historic sites and cultural landmarks.

For outdoor lovers, Tallahassee and its surroundings provide an abundance of natural beauty. Towering pines, sprawling live oaks draped in Spanish moss, and clear, spring-fed rivers define the landscape. Wakulla Springs State Park, home to one of the deepest and largest freshwater springs in the world, offers a refreshing escape into Florida's natural wonders, while the St. Marks National Wildlife Refuge is one of the best places in the state for birdwatching, wildlife viewing, and coastal hiking.

This section of the book highlights the best day trips within a two-hour round-trip drive of Tallahassee, helping you uncover the wild, unspoiled Florida that still exists today. Whether you're looking for a shaded hiking trail, a peaceful kayak trip, a freshwater spring, or a historic small town, these destinations will give you a taste of the Florida that isn't in the brochures. So grab a map, take the back roads, and get ready to explore the hidden beauty of North Florida.

Tallahassee, Florida

Total day trip time: approximately 4 hours. 10-minute round-trip drive, leaving 3 ¾ hours for fun and exploring.

Dogs: Yes (Not allowed in playground, amphitheater, or fountain area)

- **Fees:**
  - $0

(concerts and other events may have an additional fee. Check the website for events and concerts)

- **Activities:** Walking, picnicking waterplay, playground, history

Trails, Waterfalls, and Open Spaces for Every Explorer

If you want to spend time in the heart of downtown but still crave that wilderness feel, Cascades Park is the perfect place to explore. This vibrant 120-acre urban park seamlessly blends natural beauty, recreation, and history, offering a retreat where you can enjoy wide-open green spaces, shaded walking trails, and serene water features—all within steps of Tallahassee's bustling city center.

One of the most joyful and energetic spots in the park is Imagination Fountain, located on the west side of Prime Meridian Plaza. This interactive water feature boasts 73 jets that randomly shoot filtered water into the air, creating a fun, water-park atmosphere that's perfect for children eager to cool off on a warm day. Laughter fills the air as kids run through the unpredictable repellants, some fully prepared for the soaking, others caught delightfully off guard. Changing areas are conveniently located, as well as picnic tables throughout the park.

As the day fades into evening, Imagination Fountain transforms into a spectacular nighttime show. Set to music and vibrant lights, the fountain comes alive in a seven-minute water and light performance that repeats throughout the night. It's a mesmerizing sight that adds a touch of magic to the park's ambiance. For those planning a visit, it's important to note that the fountain may occasionally be closed for maintenance, so checking ahead is always a good idea.

Beyond the water's edge, Discovery Playscape offers another exciting space designed just for kids. Built with natural materials and creative play structures, this thoughtfully crafted playground encourages children to climb, jump, explore, and let their imaginations run wild. Among its many features are the Cypress Climb, Steephead Slide, Log Jump, Butterfly Garden, and Beach Sand area, each offering unique ways for kids to engage with nature while enjoying an active day outdoors. Whether they're balancing on logs, sliding through tunnels, or digging in the sand, children will find endless opportunities for adventure in this playful corner of the park.

For visitors seeking a more peaceful, scenic experience, Cascades Park offers miles of beautifully paved trails that wind through lush green spaces, serene ponds, and shaded pathways. These trails provide a perfect escape for walkers, joggers, and cyclists alike, allowing visitors to enjoy a leisurely stroll, a brisk morning run, or a refreshing bike ride through the park's natural beauty. The three main trails with a total of 2.3 miles of interconnected paths offer the ideal setting for an afternoon spent outdoors, whether you're exercising, unwinding, or simply soaking in the sights and sounds of nature. Even though you're in the center of downtown Tallahassee, the abundance of trees, water features, and wildlife creates a peaceful retreat that feels miles away from the city's hustle and bustle.

Beyond its play areas and scenic trails, Cascades Park is steeped in history, offering visitors a chance to connect with Florida's past while enjoying its present beauty. The park is home to several significant landmarks, including the Prime Meridian Marker, a historic site marking the starting point for all land surveys in Florida. Scattered throughout the park are memorials and monuments honoring veterans, civil rights leaders, and Tallahassee's rich cultural heritage.

Hours	Park: 24/7 Interactive Play: 9:00 a.m. - 8:00 p.m. daily
Phone	850-891-3866
Location	1001 S Gadsden St, Tallahassee, FL 32301
Website	talgov.com/parks/parks-cascades

Suggested Supplies

Water	Snacks	Change of clothes for kids if playing in water.
Picnic supplies	Waste clean-up bags for Fido	Water shoes/ towels for kids

Lake Jackson Mounds Archaeological State Park

Tallahassee, Florida

Total day trip time: approximately3 ½ hours. 30-minute round-trip drive, leaving 3 hours for a pleasant walk to explore the area.
Dogs: Yes

- **Fees:**
  - $3.00 per vehicle. Please use the honor box to pay fees. Correct change is required. Limit 8 people per vehicle.
  - $2.00 pedestrians, bicyclists, extra passengers, passengers in vehicle with holder of Annual Individual Entrance Pass.
- **Activities**: birding, hiking, picnicking, fishing, wildlife viewing.

Step Into Florida's Ancient Past Where History and Nature Unite

This historic park is home to six of the seven known earthen temple mounds built by the Native peoples of the region, with two mounds open for public viewing. These impressive structures provide a glimpse into the prehistoric societies that once thrived along the shores of Lake Jackson.

For those looking to explore beyond the mounds, the park offers two scenic trails. The interpretive trail takes visitors through remnants of Florida's Territorial Period and early statehood (1820–1860) when the land was part of a grand estate owned by Colonel Robert Butler. The nature trail winds through a sandhill habitat, home to a variety of native plants and trees. Along the way, hikers can spot the remains of a 19th-century grist mill, a reminder of the area's early agricultural past.

For wildlife enthusiasts and birdwatchers, Lake Jackson provides ample opportunities to observe native species in their natural habitat. Whether you're here for history, hiking, or a peaceful picnic, Lake Jackson Mounds Archaeological State Park offers a unique blend of cultural heritage and natural beauty just minutes from Tallahassee. Guided tours are available upon request.

Hours	8 a.m. to sundown, 365 days a year
Phone	850-487-7989
Location	3600 Indian Mounds Road Tallahassee FL 32303
Website	floridastateparks.org/parks-and-trails/lake-jackson-mounds-archaeological-state-park

Suggested Supplies

Water	Snacks	Bug repellant
Sunscreen	Stroller or wagon for kids	Waste clean-up bags for Fido
Picnic supplies	Binoculars	Picnic blanket/chairs

Tallahassee, Florida

Total day trip time: approximately.4 ½ hours. 30-minute round-trip drive, leaving 4 hours for fun and exploring.

Dogs: Yes

- **Fees:**
  - $6.00 per vehicle (up to eight people). *Does not include gardens entry, January through April.*
  - $4.00 single-occupant vehicle.
  - $2.00 pedestrians, bicyclists, extra passengers, passengers in vehicle with holder of Annual Individual Entrance Pass.
  - $6.00 **garden entry:** Adults during blooming months (January through April).
  - $3.00 **garden entry:** Children ages 2 to 12 during blooming months (January through April).
  - **Single kayak or paddleboard**
    - $20.00 per hour/$50 full day
  - **Tandem kayak**
    - $40 .00per hour/$80 full day
- **Activities**: Bicycling, fishing, paddling, walking/hiking, swimming, wildlife viewing

Tranquil Trails, Reflecting Pools, and Southern Charm Await

Tucked away in the northern part of Tallahassee, Alfred B. Maclay Gardens State Park is a breathtaking retreat featuring 28 acres of historic ornamental gardens designed by Alfred B. Maclay himself. This meticulously crafted landscape offers a walled garden, a reflection pool, Black Pond, and a secluded hidden garden, each providing a peaceful escape into nature's beauty. The lakeside pavilion overlooking Lake Hall is the perfect place to sit with a book, soak in the view, and enjoy the serenity of this special place.

Beyond the gardens, the park offers 11 miles of scenic trails in the Lake Overstreet portion, perfect for hiking, jogging, biking, or horseback riding. As you explore, keep an eye out for local wildlife, including American alligators, great blue herons, and bald eagles. If you visit between October and mid-May, you may even catch a glimpse of nesting bald eagles caring for their young.

With majestic oaks, vibrant flora, and abundant wildlife, Maclay Gardens is a favorite destination for photographers and nature lovers alike. The park also offers kayak and mountain bike rentals, allowing visitors to paddle on the 144-acre freshwater lake or tackle nearly six miles of off-road, single-track mountain biking trails in the western portion of the park. A five-mile, double-loop, shared-use trail winds through the hardwood forests and follows historic natural-surfaced roads, providing a variety of terrain for outdoor enthusiasts.

Whether you're looking to stroll through blooming gardens, paddle across a peaceful lake, spot wildlife, or take on a challenging bike trail, Maclay Gardens offers a little bit of everything—all within a short drive from downtown Tallahassee.

Hours	The park and the historic gardens are open 8 a.m. until sunset daily. The Maclay House museum is open January through April, 9 a.m. until 5 p.m. daily.
Phone	850-245-2157
Location	3540 Thomasville Road Tallahassee FL 32309
Website	floridastateparks.org/index.php/MaclayGardens/

Suggested Supplies

Water	Sunscreen	Binoculars
Walking shoes	Water shoes	Wagon for small children
Bug repellant	Snacks	Waste clean-up bags for Fido

Tallahassee, Florida

Total day trip time: approximately 5 hours. 30-minute round-trip drive, leaving 4 ½ hours for fun, adventure, and exploring.

Dogs: No

- **Fees:**
  - General Admission:
    - $15.50 Adults
    - $14.50 Seniors (65+)
    - $14.50 College Students (w/I.D.)
    - $11.00 Children (4-15)
    - $0 Children (3 and under) and members
  - **Treemendous Adventures** (children 41" to 60" tall)
    - $19.00 Member
    - $21.00 Non-Member
  - **Canopy Crossing** (Must be at least 54" tall)
    - $40.00 Member
    - $43.00 Non-Member
  - **Soaring Cypress** (Must be at least 54" tall)
    - $50.00 Member ~
    - $55.00 Non-Member
- **Activities**: Walking/hiking, history, Zipline, wildlife viewing

Where Nature, History, and Adventure Meet

At first glance, it might seem unusual to include a museum in a book about outdoor adventures—but the Tallahassee Museum is anything but ordinary. Set on 52 acres of woodlands along the scenic shores of Lake Bradford, this open-air museum blends nature, history, wildlife, and adventure, making it one of the most unique destinations in North Florida.

Here, you can stroll along boardwalks, spotting native Florida wildlife like black bears, deer, red wolves, and panthers in naturalistic habitats. You can explore historic buildings that bring two centuries of North Florida's history to life, from an 1880s farmstead to a Civil Rights-era schoolhouse. If you're looking for a thrill, you can strap on a harness and soar through the treetops on one of the museum's zipline and aerial adventure courses. And if all that adventure works up an appetite, you can grab a bite at the café or stop by the Museum Store to browse local art and gifts.

The Tallahassee Museum is a place to see, explore, and experience—whether you're wandering nature trails, stepping into the past, or climbing into the trees. It's where education meets adventure, making it a perfect day trip for anyone looking to combine history, wildlife, and outdoor fun in one unforgettable visit.

Hours	9 am – 5 pm: Monday-Saturday 11 am – 5 pm: Sunday Closed: Thanksgiving, Christmas Eve, Christmas Day and New Year's Day
Phone	850-575-8684
Location	3945 Museum Drive Tallahassee, FL 32310-6325
Website	tallahasseemuseum.org/

Suggested Supplies

Comfortable shoes/clothing	Water	Snacks
Bug repellant	Sunscreen	

Wakulla Springs, Florida

Total day trip time: approximately 5 hours. 30-minute round-trip drive, leaving 4 ½ hours for fun and exploring.

Dogs: Yes

- **Fees:**
  - Admission
    - $6.00 vehicle with two to eight occupants.
    - $4.00 single-occupant vehicle.
    - $2.00 per extra vehicle occupant.
    - $2.00 pedestrian or bicyclist.
  - **River Boat Tours**
    - $8.00 ages 13 years and up.
    - $5.00 ages 3 to 12 years.
    - $0 ages 3 years and under.

Tickets are available by **reservation only**; call **850-421-2000**.

- **Activities**: Bicycling, bird watching, wildlife viewing, boat tours, hiking, picnicking, swimming.

Step Into Old Florida at One of the World's Largest Freshwater Springs

One of the world's largest and deepest freshwater springs, Wakulla Springs is a place where nature, history, and adventure come together. The sapphire-blue waters, rimmed by an ancient cypress swamp, are home to manatees, alligators, and an incredible variety of wildlife that can be spotted from a riverboat tour or the diving platform.

With a constant temperature of 70 degrees, the spring offers a refreshing escape on even the hottest summer days. Towering cypress trees draped in Spanish moss create an atmosphere that feels untouched by time, making Wakulla Springs the perfect setting for classic Hollywood films like Tarzan's Secret Treasure (1941) and Creature from the Black Lagoon (1954).

Long before the cameras arrived, early Native Americans called this area home, establishing villages along the shoreline. Today, visitors can swim where mastodons once roamed, paddle waters once traveled by dugout canoes, and take guided boat tours through the same jungle-like landscape that has existed for thousands of years.

The park is also home to the historic Wakulla Springs Lodge, a beautifully preserved 1930s Spanish-style retreat. Inside, you'll find original period furniture, a vintage elevator, and intricately painted ceilings that showcase scenes of Florida's rich wildlife and history.

Hours	8 a.m. until sundown, 365 days a year.
Phone	850-561-7276
Location	465 Wakulla Park Drive Wakulla Springs FL 32327
Website	floridastateparks.org/WakullaSprings

Suggested Supplies

Water	Snacks	Activity-appropriate clothing and shoes
Towels	Water shoes	Picnic and supplies
Waste clean-up bags for Fido	Sunscreen	Bug repellant
Old picnic blanket/chairs	Binoculars	Picnic blanket/chairs

Tallahassee, Florida

Total day trip time: approximately 4 hours. 40-minute drive round trip, leaving 2 ½ hours for a leisurely stroll.
Dogs: Yes
- **Fees:**
  - $0
- **Activities**: Walking, playground, wildlife viewing, birdwatching

A Hidden Haven of Trails, Wildlife, and Serene Wetlands

Spanning more than 750 acres, the St. Marks Headwaters Greenway is a beautifully preserved natural area that offers a peaceful escape into Florida's wetlands. Explore three miles of pedestrian and bike-friendly trails, which wind through the landscape via boardwalks, scenic overlooks, and a bridge that offers stunning views of the surrounding wetlands. The greenway also features picnic shelters, restrooms, and shaded seating areas, making it an ideal spot for a leisurely afternoon outdoors.

Hours	Dawn till dusk, seven days a week.
Phone	850-606-1470
Location	640 Baum Rd, Tallahassee, Florida
Website	cms.leoncountyfl.gov/Government/Departments/Resource-Stewardship/Parks-Recreation/Park-Index?park-id=14178

Suggested Supplies

Water	Snacks	Stroller or wagon for children
Sunscreen	Bug repellant	Comfortable shoes
Waste clean-up bags for Fido	Binoculars	

Crawfordville, Florida

Total day trip time: approximately 1-hour drive round trip, leaving 3 ½ hours for hiking and viewing.
Dogs: Yes
- **Fees:**
  - $0
- **Activities**: Hiking, wildlife viewing

A Hidden Sanctuary of Ancient Palms and Untamed Beauty

Winding through coastal swamps, towering palms, and ancient oaks, this 5.3-mile hike in St. Marks National Wildlife Refuge is one of the most breathtaking and unique sections of the Florida Trail south of Tallahassee. The highlight of the journey is Shepherd Spring, a third-magnitude spring tucked deep within the dense floodplain forest—but getting there is just as rewarding as the destination.

The hike begins with an easy walk along forest roads, but soon leads into the Cathedral of Palms, a remarkable hammock where towering cabbage palms grow in dense, cathedral-like formations. As the trail skirts the coastal estuary, the landscape shifts dramatically—when tides are high, the trail itself becomes submerged, and hikers may find themselves wading through shallow waters beneath the swaying palms.

For more than a mile and a half, the Florida Trail follows a tree-lined forest road flanked by vast cypress swamps. Water drains across the footpath in several places, making for a muddy, sometimes slippery trek, and bridges can be slick after rain. As the forest thickens, ancient oaks twist among the palms, adding to the landscape's wild beauty.

At 2.8 miles, a sign and bench mark the turnoff to Shepherd Spring, where a short path leads to a clear, deep spring, often visited by a resident alligator. A nearby bench provides a quiet resting spot to soak in the untouched beauty of this hidden oasis.

From the spring, the trail continues through bamboo thickets, weaving beneath pines, oaks, and Southern magnolias before passing Wakulla Field Campsite, the only designated campsite along this section of the trail. The final stretch crosses another swamp forest, eventually reconnecting with the forest road before leading to Spring Creek Highway, where a blue-blazed side trail marks the route to the trailhead.

Challenging, scenic, and immersive, this hike offers a true taste of wild Florida, where every step brings new discoveries—from pristine estuaries and towering palms to hidden springs and ancient oaks. If you're looking for a memorable trek off the beaten path, the Cathedral of Palms and Shepherd Spring will not disappoint.

Special Directions

This hike is located in the Wakulla Unit of St. Marks National Wildlife Refuge. Before heading out, check the refuge website or call ahead to confirm hunt dates in the fall and winter, as it's safest to plan your hike outside of active hunting seasons.

To reach the trailhead, turn south onto Wakulla Beach Road from U.S. 98 (Coastal Highway). This unpaved road can become seasonally wet and muddy, so check conditions if traveling after heavy rain. When you pass the refuge boundary sign, look for a small parking area on the right. Be mindful not to block the gate.

The hike follows the Florida Trail, marked with orange blazes, along Refuge Road 200 for 1.7 miles before turning off the main road. As you continue along the orange-blazed trail, the landscape changes— towering cabbage palms and slash pines grow in dense formations, signaling your entrance into the Cathedral of Palms.

After about one mile, you'll reach a blue-blazed junction. Follow the blue trail for a short walk to Shepherd Spring, a small but stunning freshwater spring that feeds into Goose Creek Bay. Alligators are commonly seen here, so use caution near the water's edge.

Hours	Daylight to dusk
Phone	850-925-6121
Location	3102 Spring Creek Hwy, Crawfordville, FL 32327
Website	fws.gov/refuge/st-marks

Suggested Supplies

Water (no fresh water available on site)	Bug repellant	Hiking boots (the trail can be muddy)
Waste clean-up bags for Fido	Snacks (no food available)	Sunscreen
Binoculars		

Monticello, Florida

Total day trip time: approximately 3 hours. 1 ½-hour drive round trip, leaving 2 hours for fun and animal adventure.

Dogs: No

- **Fees:**
    o $15.00 per person.
    o $0 Children 3 & Under
- **Activities:** Animal petting, train and wagon rides, corn maze, corn pit, and more family fun.

A Family-Friendly Escape Filled with Furry and Feathered Friends

Aunt Louise's Farm is home to a delightful mix of friendly animals, including alpacas, donkeys, ducks, emus, geese, goats, Highland cows, horses, peacocks, pigs, quail, rabbits, a tortoise, turkeys, and even zebu! Whether you're an animal lover, an outdoor enthusiast, or just looking for a fun, family-friendly outing, our farm is the perfect place to make memories and start traditions.

Every season brings something special to Aunt Louise's Farm, and there's no better time to visit than during Fall Farm Days and the Spring Wildflower Festival.

As autumn rolls in, the farm comes alive with the sights and sounds of Fall Farm Days. Families pile into wagon rides for a scenic trip around the farm, while excited kids climb aboard the barrel train, ready for a bumpy, laughter-filled ride. At the rubber duck race, little ones cheer as their ducks bob down the waterway, hoping theirs will reach the finish line first. The farm's famous corn maze challenges visitors to find their way through towering stalks of golden corn, while the corn pit— a giant sandbox filled with dried corn kernels—offers endless fun for children eager to dive in. Of course, no trip to the farm is complete without meeting the friendly animals, where visitors can pet and interact with goats, alpacas, donkeys, pigs, and more. And just when you think the fun is over, there are even more fall-themed activities waiting to be discovered!

When spring arrives, the farm transforms once again for the Spring Wildflower Festival. Visitors are welcomed by fields bursting with color, as vibrant wildflowers sway in the breeze, creating the perfect backdrop for a relaxing stroll or a family photo. The wagon rides and barrel train make their return, carrying guests around the farm to take in the fresh spring air. Kids eagerly gather around for another round of rubber duck races, while the farm animals soak up the sunshine and enjoy the company of their new visitors. Whether it's wandering through the wildflowers, making memories with the animals, or simply enjoying a beautiful day outdoors, the Spring Wildflower Festival is a magical way to welcome the season.

Whether you're here for fall festivities, springtime blooms, or just to enjoy a day on the farm, Aunt Louise's Farm is a must-visit destination for wholesome family fun!

Hours	The farm is open seasonally, so be sure to check the website before planning your trip.
Phone	850.251.7708
Location	8101 Waukeenah Hwy Monticello, FL 32344
Website	auntlouisesfarm.com/

Suggested Supplies

Water	Snacks	Dirt-acceptable clothing and shoes
Close-toed shoes	Wipes (handy to have your own!)	Bug repellant

Monticello, Florida

Total day trip time: approximately 6 ½ hours. 1 ½-hour drive round trip, leaving 5 hours for paddling, riding, and exploring.
Dogs: Yes

- **Fees:**
  - **Airboat Tours:** $125.00 for 2 people and $25.00 for each additional person
  - **Canoe and Kayak Rental** Rates (Boat rentals include whistle, paddles and life jackets)
    - $30.00 **Canoe & Single Kayak** Daily
    - $40.00 **Double Kayak** Daily
    - $40.00 **Paddle Board** Daily
- **Activities**: Boating, fishing, birdwatching, wildlife viewing, airboat tours

Drift, Paddle, or Speed Through One of Florida's Hidden Gems

For those seeking a peaceful, scenic escape, the spring-fed waters of the Wacissa River provide the perfect setting for adventure. This stunning waterway, fed by numerous freshwater springs, offers a gentle, relaxing canoe or kayak trip through some of Florida's most untouched natural beauty. Whether you're looking to spend the day exploring, enjoy a riverside picnic, or take a refreshing swim in the clear, cool waters, the Wacissa delivers an unforgettable outdoor experience.

For those craving a little more speed and excitement, airboat tours offer a thrilling way to explore the river's hidden corners. Glide across glass-like waters, weave through cypress stands, and experience the river from a whole new perspective. Airboat guides often know the best spots for wildlife encounters, making these tours an incredible way to see Florida's natural wonders up close.

Fishing enthusiasts will also find plenty to love here. The Wacissa is home to bream, small and largemouth bass, mullet, and catfish. Bring a fishing pole, some worms, crickets, or your favorite lure, and you're set for a great day of casting and catching. If you're looking for the best fishing spots, calling ahead for a local fishing report is always a smart idea.

Birdwatchers and wildlife lovers will be in awe of the rich biodiversity that thrives along the Wacissa. The river is a haven for aquatic birds and native wildlife, including bald eagles, egrets, herons, osprey, wood storks, and barred owls. As you paddle or ride along, you might also spot alligators, river otters, turtles, and countless other species in their natural habitat.

Whether you're here to canoe, kayak, fish, take a scenic airboat ride, or simply soak in the tranquility, the Wacissa River offers an unforgettable glimpse into Old Florida's wild and pristine beauty.

Hours	8 a.m. to 8 p.m. 7 days a week
Phone	850-997-5023 or 850-545-2895
Location	290 Wacissa Springs Rd. Monticello, Florida 32344
Website	wacissarivercanoerentals.com

Suggested Supplies

Water	Snacks	Bug repellant
Water shoes/old sneakers	Waterproof bags (ziplock bags will work)	Waste clean-up bags for Fido
Binoculars		

Dr. Julian G. Bruce St. George Island State Park

St. George Island, Florida

Total day trip time: approximately 6 hours. 2-hour drive round trip, leaving 4 hours for fun and exploring.

Dogs: Yes: Pets are not permitted on beaches, boardwalks, or playgrounds

- **Fees:**
  - $6.00 per vehicle (two to eight people).
  - $4.00 single-occupant vehicle.
  - $2.00 pedestrians, bicyclists, extra passengers, passengers in vehicle with holder of Annual Individual Entrance Pass.
- **Activities:** Hiking, bicycling, birding, paddling (rentals available at ranger station), swimming (no lifeguard).

Escape the Crowds and Discover the Quiet Magic of St. George Island

Located on a barrier island along the shores of historic Apalachicola Bay, St. George Island State Park is a slice of untouched paradise. With miles of undeveloped beaches, this park is a haven for beachgoers, birdwatchers, and anglers—offering breathtaking Gulf sunsets and some of the best stargazing in the Panhandle.

On the Gulf side, you'll find crystal-clear waters, soft white sand, and endless opportunities for sunbathing, swimming, and fishing. If you're lucky, you might even catch a glimpse of dolphins playing just offshore.

The bay side of the island is a completely different world, where thriving marshlands shelter wading birds and abundant saltwater fish. Nature trails weave through scrublands and pine forests, home to red-cockaded woodpeckers, bald eagles, and five-lined skinks—brilliant blue lizards that dart through the underbrush.

St. George Island is also one of the best places for shelling and beachcombing, with an ever-changing shoreline rich in coastal treasures. During the summer months, the park becomes a nesting ground for sea turtles and shorebirds such as snowy plovers, least terns, willets, and black skimmers.

Whether you're here to hike, paddle, fish, camp, or simply relax, St. George Island State Park offers the perfect balance of adventure and tranquility—a rare, unspoiled gem on Florida's Forgotten Coast.

Hours	8 a.m. until sundown, 365 days a year.
Phone	850-927-2111
Location	1900 E. Gulf Beach Drive St. George Island FL 32328
Website	floridastateparks.org/parks-and-trails/dr-julian-g-bruce-st-george-island-state-park

Suggested Supplies

Water	Snacks/picnic	Bug repellant
Sunscreen	Blanket/chairs	Waste clean-up bags for Fido
Beach toys	Beach umbrella	Towels
Water shoes	Change of clothes	Sunglasses

Marianna, Florida

Total day trip time: approximately 7 hours. 2 ½-hour drive round trip, leaving 4 ½ hours for fun and exploring.

Dogs: Yes (**Not allowed on cave tour**)

- **Fees:**
  - $5.00 per vehicle
  - **Cave tours:**
    - $0.00 Children 2 and under
    - $8.00 Ages 3 to 12
    - $15.00 Ages 13 and up:
- **Activities**: Cave tour, hiking, boating, swimming, picnicking, fishing, wildlife viewing, birdwatching

Above and Below: Hike, Paddle, and Discover Florida's Only Tour Cave

Best known for its highly decorated tour cave, Florida Caverns State Park offers visitors a chance to explore Florida's only air-filled, walk-through cave system. But while the mystical underground formations are a must-see, there's much more to discover above ground. From winding hiking trails and scenic river paddling to picnic spots and family-friendly recreation areas, this park offers an unforgettable experience for adventurers of all kinds.

Step into an otherworldly underground realm, where cool air, the gentle sound of dripping water, and breathtaking rock formations surround you. The guided cave tour takes visitors through a dozen large underground rooms, revealing stalactites, stalagmites, flowstones, and draperies that have formed over thousands of years. The pathways, carefully carved out by the Civilian Conservation Corps in the 1930s, display the chisel marks of workers who made this hidden underground world accessible.

Before starting the tour, visitors are briefed on safety precautions, as some sections require stooping to pass through low ceilings (as low as 4.5 feet for short distances), navigating narrow passages, and descending staircases. Inside, the caverns remain at a constant 65 degrees year-round, a refreshing break from Florida's warm climate. Along the way, explorers may even encounter bats, cave crickets, salamanders, and other cave-dwelling wildlife.

After the tour, guests emerge from the cave into a lush hardwood forest, where the adventure continues.

While Florida Caverns is famous for its caves, it also boasts approximately seven miles of multi-use trails that weave through towering hardwood forests and scenic floodplains. These trails offer beautiful nature walks, birdwatching opportunities, and glimpses of Florida's diverse ecosystems.

For those who prefer water adventures, the Chipola River provides a beautiful, tranquil setting for canoeing and kayaking. Visitors can bring their own canoe or rent one from the park, paddling upriver to discover hidden springs and spot local wildlife.

Beyond the caves, trails, and river, visitors can also enjoy swimming in the designated areas, or taking a canoe upriver (rentals available).

Whether you're drawn to the otherworldly beauty of the caves, the tranquility of a river paddle, or the peaceful charm of a picnic under the trees, Florida Caverns State Park offers something for everyone. With its mix of underground wonder and outdoor adventure, it's one of Florida's most unique and unforgettable destinations—a place where nature, history, and exploration come together.

Hours	Park: 8 a.m. until sundown, 365 days a year. Cave tours: seven days a week from 9 a.m.-4 p.m. CST.
Phone	850-482-1228
Location	3345 Caverns Road Marianna FL 32446
Website	floridastateparks.org/parks-and-trails/florida-caverns-state-park

Suggested Supplies

Water	Snacks	Bug repellant
Waste clean-up bags for Fido	Light jacket or sweatshirt for cave tour	Sneakers or hiking boots for cave tour
Picnic supplies (grills available—first come, first served)		

Gainesville

Nestled in the heart of North Central Florida, Gainesville is more than just a lively college town—it's a gateway to some of the state's most spectacular natural wonders. Within an hour's drive, you can find crystal-clear springs, winding rivers, dense forests, rolling prairies, and hidden trails that offer adventure in every direction. Whether you're looking to paddle through the cool, turquoise waters of a spring-fed river, hike beneath towering live oaks draped in Spanish moss, or spot wildlife in one of Florida's last remaining savannas, the Gainesville area is packed with outdoor experiences that showcase the state's wild beauty.

For water lovers, the region is home to some of Florida's most famous springs and rivers. Ichetucknee Springs, Ginnie Springs, and Blue Springs offer stunning places to swim, snorkel, and tube, while the Santa Fe River provides an ideal spot for kayaking or canoeing past lush, undeveloped shorelines. The water here is so clear that you can see fish, turtles, and even the occasional manatee gliding below.

If you prefer to stay on land, hiking and wildlife watching opportunities abound. Paynes Prairie Preserve State Park, just south of Gainesville, is a vast, open savanna where wild bison and wild horses still roam—one of the only places in Florida where you can see such creatures in the wild. Devil's Millhopper Geological State Park offers a chance to descend into a prehistoric sinkhole, where a lush, rainforest-like environment hides in the depths of a collapsed limestone cavern. Nearby, the San Felasco Hammock Preserve and Sweetwater Wetlands Park provide miles of shaded trails and boardwalks, perfect for spotting deer, armadillos, otters, and an incredible variety of birds.

For those who enjoy scenic drives, the area's rural backroads wind through canopied oak tunnels, rolling farmland, and charming small towns, making for a peaceful escape from city life. If you're up for an underground adventure, the region is also home to some of Florida's most fascinating caves, including the Limestone Caves of Warren Cave Nature Preserve, one of the largest dry caves in the state.

This section of the book highlights the best day trips within an hour of Gainesville, helping you uncover the hidden side of Florida—one where the water is clear, the trails are quiet, and nature is just waiting to be explored. So, lace up your hiking boots, grab your paddle, or pack a picnic, and let's dive into the wild beauty that surrounds Gainesville.

Gainesville, Florida

Total day trip time: approximately 3 hours. 15-minute round-trip drive, leaving 2 ¾ hours for fun and exploring.
Dogs: Yes
* **Fees:**
  o $4.00 per vehicle
  o $2.00 for pedestrians and bicyclists.
* **Activities**: nature walk, sinkhole exploration, picnicking.

Lush, Cool, and Mysterious—Explore a Hidden Rainforest Below the Surface

Amidst North Florida's sandy terrain and towering pine forests, an unexpected wonder awaits—a massive, bowl-shaped sinkhole plunging 120 feet into a lush, miniature rainforest. Water trickles down the steep limestone walls, vanishing into crevices in the earth, while dense vegetation flourishes in the cool, shaded environment, even during the driest summers.

This natural phenomenon has provided a glimpse into Florida's prehistoric past. Fossilized shark teeth, marine shells, and the remains of extinct land animals discovered within the sinkhole have offered valuable insight into the state's geological and ecological history.

Visitors should be prepared for a workout, as exploring this unique landscape requires descending and climbing numerous stairs—but the reward is an otherworldly escape into one of Florida's most intriguing natural wonders.

Hours	8:00 a.m. to sundown daily
Phone	352-955-2008
Location	4732 Millhopper Road Gainesville FL 32653
Website	floridastateparks.org/parks-and-trails/devils-millhopper-geological-state-park

Suggested Supplies

Water	Snacks	Bug repellant
Waste clean-up bags for Fido	Sneakers or hiking boots	Sunscreen

Williston, Florida

Total day trip time: approximately 2 ½ hours. 30- minute drive round trip, leaving 2 hours for the tour.

Dogs: No

- **Fees:**
  - $10.00 Child (under 2 free)
  - $20.00 Adult
  - $5.00 **Hand feeding elephants**
  - $40.00 **elephant ride** (per person)
  - $25.00 **photo op**
- **Activities**: Wildlife viewing and education

A One-of-a-Kind Sanctuary for an Unforgettable Elephant Encounter

Deep in the heart of Florida, Two Tails Ranch is a truly unique destination—one of the only privately owned elephant facilities in the country. Since its founding in 1984, the ranch has provided a safe and caring environment for both Asian and African elephants, offering sanctuary to those in need of retirement, medical care, or temporary housing. Over the years, more than 250 elephants have called the ranch home, making it a place where these gentle giants can be observed, studied, and appreciated up close.

Visitors to Two Tails Ranch are treated to a rare and unforgettable experience, where they can stand mere feet away from these massive creatures, watch them interact, and even feed them. Guided tours provide fascinating insight into elephant behavior, conservation challenges, and the intricate care required to support such enormous and intelligent animals. For those looking for an even closer encounter, the ranch offers elephant rides and other hands-on experiences that bring guests face-to-face with the world's largest land mammals.

Beyond elephants, the ranch is also home to a variety of other exotic animals, including zebras, ostriches, emus, tortoises, camels, and playful ring-tailed lemurs. These diverse residents add to the experience, offering visitors a chance to connect with an array of fascinating wildlife in a peaceful, natural setting.

Whether it's watching an elephant enjoy a mud bath, hearing the deep rumble of their vocalizations, or learning about their vital role in ecosystems around the world, a visit to Two Tails Ranch is both awe-inspiring and deeply educational.

For wildlife lovers, families, and anyone fascinated by these magnificent creatures, Two Tails Ranch offers an up-close encounter unlike any other, providing a once-in-a-lifetime opportunity to connect with elephants in a way few places can offer.

Hours	Educational tours are available Monday, Tuesday, Wednesday, Friday, Saturday, and Sunday **by appointment only. Call or email:** (pzerbini@allaboutelephants.com) **Closed on Thursdays.**
Phone	352-528-6585
Location	18655 NE 81st St, Williston, FL 32696
Website	allaboutelephants.com/

Suggested Supplies

Water	Bug repellant	Stroller or wagon for children
Sunglasses	Sunscreen	Comfortable shoes (close-toed suggested)

Gainesville, Florida

Total day trip time: approximately3 ½ hours. 20-minute drive round trip, leaving 3+ hours for fun and exploring.
Dogs: No
- **Fees:** $0
- **Activities:** wildlife viewing, birding, hiking, wildflower viewing, historical information

Where Wildflower Trails Meet Living History

A hidden gem in Gainesville, Morningside Nature Center is the city's premier nature park and one of the last remaining examples of fire-dependent longleaf pine woodlands in the region. Spanning more than 260 acres, this protected natural area is home to an incredible diversity of plant and animal life. With over six miles of scenic trails, visitors can explore sandhill ecosystems, pine flatwoods, cypress domes, and actively restored native habitats. In spring and summer, Morningside bursts into color, boasting one of the area's most spectacular wildflower displays, attracting pollinators, birds, and nature enthusiasts alike.

But Morningside is more than just a nature preserve—it's also a living connection to Florida's past. The Living History Farm transports visitors back to the 1870s, bringing Florida Cracker family life to life through interactive demonstrations. On Living History Days (the first Saturday of the month, September through May), staff and volunteers demonstrate traditional farm chores and activities, offering a glimpse into the daily rhythms of early Florida settlers.

One of the park's most beloved traditions is the Annual Cane Boil and Fiddle Fest, held every year on the Saturday of Thanksgiving. This festival blends history, music, and heritage, as visitors gather to watch fresh sugarcane juice being boiled down into syrup, just as it was done generations ago. The event also hosts the Longleaf Pine Youth Fiddle Contest, celebrating the folk music traditions of the South, filling the air with the lively sounds of fiddles, storytelling, and old-time melodies.

Whether you're hiking through the towering longleaf pines, spotting wildlife in a cypress dome, or stepping back in time at the Living History Farm, Morningside Nature Center offers a rare blend of outdoor adventure and cultural heritage—a perfect place to experience both the wild and historic heart of North Florida.

Hours	**Park Hours** March 15—September 30: 7 a.m.—8 p.m. daily October 1—March 14: 7 a.m.—6 p.m. daily **Living History Farm Hours** 9 a.m.-4:30 p.m. Monday-Saturday, Closed Sundays
Phone	352-334-5000
Location	3540 E University Ave, Gainesville 32641
Website	gainesvillefl.gov/Parks/Morningside-Nature-Center

Suggested Supplies

Comfortable walking shoes	Picnic supplies	Water
Snacks	Binoculars	Bug repellant
Sunscreen		

Carson Springs Wildlife Conservation Foundation

Gainesville, Florida

Total day trip time: approximately 3 or 5 hours. 45-minute drive round trip, leaving 2- or 4- hours (depending on the tour you select) for viewing and learning about the animals.

Dogs: No

- **Fees:**
  - Fees range from $10.00 children/$15.00 adult to $15.00 children/$45.00 adult.
- **Activities**: rare and exotic wildlife viewing and education

A Sanctuary for Rare and Rescued Wildlife

Carson Springs Wildlife Conservation Foundation, located in Gainesville, Florida, is a sanctuary dedicated to the care and conservation of exotic and endangered species. Situated on 275 acres of lush Florida landscape, the foundation is home to approximately 30 rare and endangered species, totaling over 100 animals.

Visitors to Carson Springs can participate in guided tours led by professional zoologists, offering an intimate and educational experience. These tours provide insights into the individual stories of the resident animals, emphasizing conservation and the importance of preserving natural habitats. Highlights include big cat feeding demonstrations and close encounters with various species, all within a beautifully maintained, park-like setting.

Carson Springs also offers special events and open houses throughout the year, providing additional opportunities for the public to engage with the animals and learn about conservation efforts. The foundation's commitment to education and preservation makes it a valuable resource for wildlife enthusiasts and a vital participant in global conservation initiatives.

Tours are available by appointment, ensuring a personalized experience for each guest. To schedule a visit, interested individuals can contact the foundation via email at **contact@cswildlife.org** or by phone at (352) 468-2827.

Hours	Walking tours are usually every Saturday at 10 a.m. Book online or via email (contact@cswildlife.org) for specific times.
Phone	352-468-2827
Location	8528 E, County Rd 225, Gainesville, FL 32609
Website	carsonspringswildlife.org/

Suggested Supplies

Water	Bug repellant	Close-toed shoes (you'll be walking on grass)
Stroller or wagon for children.	Sunscreen	Wipes (never hurts to have your own!

Micanopy, Florida

Total day trip time: approximately 4 hours. 30-minute round-trip drive, leaving 3 ½ hours for fun and exploring.

Dogs: yes (**Not allowed on La Chua, Cone's Dike or Bolen Bluff trails**)

- **Fees:**
  - **Main entrance**
    - $6.00 per vehicle (two to eight people).
    - $4.00 single-occupant vehicle.
    - $2.00 pedestrians, bicyclists, extra passengers, passengers in vehicle with holder of Annual Individual Entrance Pass.
  - **LaChua Trail** Admission
    - $4.00 per vehicle.
  - **Bolen Bluff** Admission
    - $2.00 per vehicle, limit eight people.
- **Activities:** hiking, biking, wildlife viewing, boating

From Sweeping Vistas to Hidden Trails

Paynes Prairie Preserve State Park is unlike anywhere else in Florida. This vast, 21,000-acre savanna is home to wild-roaming bison and horses, making it the only place in the state where visitors can witness these majestic animals in their natural habitat. The prairie is also a haven for nearly 300 species of birds, as well as alligators, white-tailed deer, and other native wildlife.

With eight trails weaving through the preserve, visitors can explore diverse landscapes, from open grasslands to shaded woodlands. The Gainesville-Hawthorne State Trail, a 16-mile paved path, is perfect for cycling or walking, offering a scenic journey through the park's interior. For a breathtaking perspective, the 50-foot-high observation tower provides panoramic views across the prairie, allowing visitors to spot wildlife from above.

One of the most enchanting trails in the park is Bolen Bluff, which leads hikers and cyclists through a stunning old-growth live oak forest. With towering trees draped in Spanish moss, this shady, peaceful retreat offers a striking contrast to the open prairie. The trail eventually leads to an overlook, where lucky visitors might catch a glimpse of the wild horses or bison that roam the prairie below.

A visit to Paynes Prairie is more than just a day outdoors—it's a step back in time to a Florida that once was, a landscape so rich in history that Seminole Indians once called it home. Whether you come to hike, bike, paddle, or simply take in the views, Paynes Prairie offers a wild and unforgettable experience in the heart of Florida.

If you're a fan of quaint towns or film locations, drive a little further to the town of Micanopy, where Doc Hollywood was filmed.

This park does not offer boat rentals.

Hours	8 a.m. to sundown daily
Phone	352-466-3397
Location	100 Savannah Blvd. Micanopy FL 32667
Website	floridastateparks.org/parks-and-trails/paynes-prairie-preserve-state-park

Suggested Supplies

Water	Snacks	Sunscreen
Bug repellant	Hiking boots or sneakers	Binoculars
Waste clean-up bags for Fido	Backpack	

Gainesville, Florida

Total day trip time: approximately 3 ½ hours. 20-minute round-trip drive, leaving for fun and exploring.

Dogs: No

- **Fees:**
  - $4.00 per vehicle
- **Activities:** wildlife viewing, hiking

See Dozens of Alligators Basking in Their Natural Wetland Home

One of the highlights of Paynes Prairie Preserve is the Alachua Sink -- one of the most awe-inspiring wildlife destinations in Florida. This natural limestone basin, where water from the prairie drains into underground channels, is teeming with life—and if you time your visit right, you might witness one of nature's most breathtaking gatherings: dozens, even a hundred alligators, basking together in the sun.

The sink's slow-moving waters create an ideal habitat for alligators, who lounge on the muddy banks, warming their massive bodies under the Florida sun. It's an unforgettable sight—rows of these ancient reptiles, still as statues, their scaly backs blending into the landscape, their powerful tails half-submerged in the marsh. But don't be fooled by their stillness; at any moment, one might slide effortlessly into the water, disappearing beneath the surface with barely a ripple.

Beyond the alligators, Alachua Sink is a magnet for wildlife. The surrounding wetlands attract wading birds, turtles, otters, and even the occasional wild horse or bison wandering in from the prairie. In the winter, thousands of migratory sandhill cranes fill the skies, their eerie, trumpet-like calls echoing across the landscape.

Getting to the sink is an easy and scenic walk along the La Chua Trail, a short boardwalk that leads directly to a viewing platform over the water. From this vantage point, visitors can safely observe the alligators and take in the beauty of the marshland stretching beyond.

For those looking to explore even deeper, the trail continues beyond the sink, leading into wide-open prairie where Florida's wild past still thrives. But even if you only have time for a short visit, Alachua Sink offers a rare and thrilling glimpse into a world where nature rules—and the alligators remind you who's in charge.

Note: Access this trail at Camp Ranch Road rather than the main park site. Trails may close when Alachua Lake appears.

Hours	8 a.m. to sunset daily
Phone	352-466-3397
Location	4801 Camp Ranch Road, Gainesville, FL 32641
Website	floridastateparks.org/parks-and-trails/paynes-prairie-preserve-state-park

Suggested Supplies

Water	Sneakers or hiking boots	Bug repellant
Binoculars	Snacks	Sunscreen

Gainesville, Florida

Total day trip time: approximately 3 hours. 45-minute round-trip drive, leaving 2 ¼ hours for viewing/learning.

Dogs: No

- **Fees:**
  - $10.00 Adults (13 to 59)
  - $6.00 Children (4 to 12)
  - $6.00 Seniors (60+)
- **Activities**: animal viewing/education

Up Close with Wildlife at One of the Nation's Only Teaching Zoos

On the Santa Fe College campus, the Santa Fe College Teaching Zoo is a one-of-a-kind, 10-acre zoo, making it the only zoo on a college campus accredited by the Association of Zoos and Aquariums (AZA). This unique facility is more than just a place to see animals—it's a hands-on learning environment where students in the college's prestigious Zoo Animal Technology program gain real-world experience in zoo management and animal care.

Managed by a team of ten full-time staff members and approximately 100 dedicated students, the zoo is home to over 70 species of animals, ranging from Florida natives to exotic creatures from around the world. Visitors can encounter majestic bald eagles, playful white-throated capuchin monkeys, stealthy American alligators, the rare Matschie's tree kangaroo, and lively Asian small-clawed otters. The zoo's collection also includes a variety of mammals, birds, reptiles, and amphibians, all housed in a naturally shaded environment designed to feel like a walk through the wilderness.

A quarter-mile, mulched trail winds through the wooded landscape, offering a stroller- and wheelchair-accessible path for guests of all ages to explore (I'd recommend a wagon rather than a stroller if you have one). Whether you're a wildlife enthusiast, a family looking for a fun and educational outing, or a student interested in animal conservation, the Santa Fe College Teaching Zoo provides an up-close and immersive experience with some of the planet's most fascinating creatures.

Hours	9 a.m. – 3 p.m. daily (last entry 2:30)
Phone	352-395-5633
Location	3000 NW 83 St Building Z, Gainesville, FL 32606
Website	sfcollege.edu/zoo/

Suggested Supplies

Water	Bug repellant	Sunscreen
Comfortable walking shoes	Wagon or stroller for kids	Snacks

San Felasco Hammock Preserve State Park

Alachua, Florida

Total day trip time: approximately 4 hours. 45-minute drive round trip, leaving 3+ hours for hiking and exploring.

Dogs: yes

- **Fees:**
    o $4.00 per vehicle
    o $2.00 pedestrians, bicyclists, extra passengers.
- **Activities**: hiking, biking, wildlife viewing

Explore One of Florida's Last Great Hardwood Forests

Towering hardwood trees rise from a landscape shaped by dramatic limestone outcrops and steep elevation changes, creating an ideal habitat for both rare plant life and abundant wildlife. Bobcats, white-tailed deer, gray foxes, wild turkeys, and countless songbirds roam the 18 distinct natural communities of the preserve, making it a haven for nature lovers and wildlife enthusiasts alike.

For those seeking outdoor adventure, the preserve's extensive trail system offers a variety of experiences. The southern two-thirds of the park is reserved exclusively for hikers, providing a peaceful escape into Florida's untouched wilderness. The northern third welcomes horseback riders, off-road cyclists, and hikers, winding through challenging terrain, shaded paths, and open fields of wildflowers and native grasses, all surrounded by old-growth forest. Whether trekking deep into the woods or pausing in a sunlit clearing, visitors will find a rare glimpse of Florida's wild and unspoiled beauty.

Hours	8 a.m. to sundown daily
Phone	352-955-2008
Location	13201 San Felasco Parkway Alachua FL 32615
Website	floridastateparks.org/parks-and-trails/san-felasco-hammock-preserve-state-park

Suggested Supplies

Water	Snacks	Bug repellant
Waste clean-up bags for Fido	Hiking boots or walking shoes	Sunscreen
Binoculars	Backpack	

Fort White, Florida

Total day trip time: approximately 5 hours. 2-hour round-trip drive, leaving 3 hours for swimming and floating.

Dogs: yes (not allowed in water)

- **Fees:**
  - $6.00 per vehicle (two to eight people).
  - $4.00 single-occupant vehicle.
  - $4.00 motorcycle (one or two people).
  - $2.00 pedestrians, bicyclists, extra passengers, passengers in vehicle with holder of Annual Individual Entrance Pass.
- **Activities**: Swimming, floating, picnicking

Tubing, Kayaking, and Wildlife—Experience the Magic of Ichetucknee

Ichetucknee Springs State Park is one of Florida's most treasured natural escapes—and even though it draws a crowd, especially in the summer, it remains a must-see destination for anyone craving a real connection to the wild, unspoiled beauty of the state. With its crystal-clear, spring-fed river, shaded trails, and abundant wildlife, it offers a truly magical experience that feels like stepping into old Florida.

There are two main entrances to the park, each offering a different kind of adventure. The North Entrance is home to the Ichetucknee Headspring, the official start of the Ichetucknee River and one of the most pristine spring runs in Florida. Here, you'll find cool, clear water holding steady at 72 degrees year-round, making it perfect for a refreshing swim or snorkel. Just a half-mile walk from the headspring is Blue Hole Spring, a deeper, cyan-colored spring beloved by snorkelers and scuba divers. While tubing is not allowed in this area, pool noodles and lifejackets are welcome for flotation—and you'll likely share the water with turtles, fish, and maybe even an otter.

If you're here to float lazily down the river on a tube, the South Entrance is your starting point. This is where you'll find access to rentals and tubing launches that take you along the peaceful, shaded Ichetucknee River. It's a classic summer activity for families and friends and a great way to take in the park's beauty at a leisurely pace.

For those who prefer to stay dry, the park's hiking trails offer plenty of reasons to explore on foot. The Trestle Point Trail, which runs alongside the Ichetucknee River, winds past a historic phosphate mining site and offers a shaded, pet-friendly stroll rich with native plants and wildlife. The Pine Ridge Trail showcases Florida's rare sandhill ecosystem, with towering longleaf pines and wide-open vistas.

Paddlers can access the river from the North Boat Launch, the furthest upstream put-in for kayaks, canoes, and paddleboards. The launch includes a kayak cradle for easy entry into the water. From there, you'll float through serene, undeveloped surroundings where herons, otters, and even manatees might make an appearance.

Because this park is so popular—especially on hot summer weekends and holidays—it's important to arrive early. The North Entrance parking lot often fills up quickly, and **entry is first-come, first-served.** Even if you've pre-purchased a day-use pass, it doesn't guarantee entry or let you skip the line at the ranger station.

Yes, Ichetucknee can get busy, but its natural beauty, crystal waters, and sense of timelessness make it well worth the visit. Come early, plan ahead, and whether you're swimming, tubing, paddling, or hiking—you'll find that Ichetucknee Springs still offers one of the most unforgettable day trip experiences in Florida.

Notes: Tube rentals are available on site. Please call or check the state park website for rules and prohibited items. Kayaks, paddleboards, and canoes are available for rent from Ichetucknee Springs. Prices range from $35 to $55, and trips range from 1 to 5 hours. Visit ichetuckneesprings.com

Hours	8 a.m. to sunset daily
Phone	386-497-4690
Location	Springs Floating 12087 S.W. U.S. Highway 27 Fort White FL 32038
Website	floridastateparks.org/parks-and-trails/ichetucknee-springs-state-park

Suggested Supplies

Water	Snacks	Picnic supplies
Bug repellant	Water shoes	Towels
Chairs/blanket (for headwater swimming/picnicking)	Change of clothes (both the river and the headwater areas have restrooms and changing area)	Hiking boots or sneakers
Waste clean-up bags for Fido	Sunscreen	Mask/snorkel

Keystone Heights, Florida

Total day trip time: approximately5 hours. 2-hour drive round trip, leaving 3 hours for swimming and exploring.

Dogs: Yes (not allowed in water)

- **Fees:**
  - $5.00 per vehicle (two to eight people).
  - $4.00 single-occupant vehicle and motorcycles.
  - $2.00 pedestrian, bicyclist, additional passengers.
- **Activities**: Swimming, hiking, birdwatching, wildlife viewing

One of Florida's First State Parks—Where History and Natural Beauty Come Together

One of Florida's first state parks, Mike Roess Gold Head Branch State Park is a testament to both natural beauty and human craftsmanship. Developed in the 1930s by the Civilian Conservation Corps (CCC), this 600-acre retreat still showcases the extraordinary artistry of the CCC, from its carefully built structures to its thoughtfully designed landscapes.

Nestled among rolling sandhills on Florida's north central ridge, Gold Head is home to one of the last remaining stands of old-growth longleaf pines—a towering reminder of the vast forests that once covered much of the region. The park's landscape is shaped by a steephead ravine, where seepage springs create the winding Gold Head Branch, a rare geological feature in Florida. Beyond the ravine, marshes, lakes, and scrubland provide habitat for a diverse array of wildlife, making this a perfect destination for birdwatching, hiking, and nature photography.

Outdoor enthusiasts can explore miles of scenic trails, including a 5.44-mile section of the Florida National Scenic Trail, which winds through the park's shaded hammocks, pine forests, and open scrublands. Along the way, hikers may spot gopher tortoises, fox squirrels, white-tailed deer, and even the occasional bald eagle soaring overhead.

For those looking to cool off or cast a fishing line, Little Lake Johnson offers opportunities for swimming, fishing, and canoeing, while the park's large picnic area, complete with tables, grills, pavilions, and a playground, makes it an ideal spot for a leisurely afternoon outdoors.

With its rich history, diverse landscapes, and wealth of outdoor activities, Mike Roess Gold Head Branch State Park is a true hidden gem, offering visitors a chance to step back in time while immersing themselves in Florida's wild and rugged beauty.

Hours	8 a.m. until sundown daily
Phone	352-316-4286
Location	6239 State Road 21 Keystone Heights FL 32656
Website	floridastateparks.org/parks-and-trails/mike-roess-gold-head-branch-state-park

Suggested Supplies

Water	Snacks	Sunscreen
Towels	Blanket/chairs	Bug repellant
Waste clean-up bags for Fido	Binoculars	Bathing suits
Change of clothes	Water shoes	Hiking boots or comfortable walking shoes

Ocala, Florida

Total day trip time: approximately 4 hours. 1 3/4-hour drive round trip, leaving 3+ hours for fun and animal interaction.

Dogs: No

- **Fees:**
  - $14.00+ tax Adults
  - $10.00+ tax Children (2-12 years old)
  - $12.00+tax Seniors
  - $11.00 +tax Veterans
  - $0 Under 2 years old
  - **Camel rides:** $14.00 (reservation and non refundable deposit required)
- **Activities:** Animal interactions

Hands-On Farm Fun for the Whole Family in the Heart of Ocala

For a fun and interactive animal experience, Petting Zoo Ocala is the perfect destination for families, animal lovers, and anyone looking to connect with friendly farm animals. This charming, family-friendly petting zoo offers an up-close encounter with a variety of gentle, well-cared-for animals, making it a great place for kids to learn about and interact with nature.

Visitors can feed, pet, and even cuddle with goats, sheep, alpacas, rabbits, donkeys, pigs, and more. The hands-on environment encourages guests to experience farm life firsthand, whether it's bottle-feeding baby animals, brushing a miniature pony, or simply watching playful goats climb their structures.

Beyond the petting zoo, the facility provides a peaceful and picturesque setting, ideal for a leisurely afternoon outdoors. Whether you're looking for a fun family outing, an educational experience for children, or just a chance to relax and enjoy the company of adorable animals, Petting Zoo Ocala is a heartwarming and unforgettable stop for animal lovers of all ages.

Hours	Monday - 10a.m. – 4 p.m. Tuesday - Closed Wednesday – Friday 10 a.m. – 4 p.m. Saturday & Sunday 10 a.m. – 5 p.m.
Phone	352-300-6688
Location	11150 FL-40, Ocala,FL,34482
Website	pettingzooocala.com

Suggested Supplies

Casual clothes (you will get dirty petting animals)	Comfortable close-toed shoes	Water
Stroller or wagon for kids	Sunscreen	Bug repellant
Wipes (never hurts to have your own)	Backpack or sling bag	Snacks

Silver Springs, Florida

Total day trip time: approximately 6 hours. 2-hour drive round trip, leaving 4 hours for fun and exploring.

Dogs: Yes (Only on trails and in picnic area. No dogs allowed on boats or in water)

- **Fees:**
  - Entrance fee: $2.00 (Children under 6-free)
  - **Glass Bottom Boat**
    - $14.00 - $30.00-30 Minute or Extended Tours.
  - **Canoe**
    - $45.00 - $85.00 - Canoes can seat up to 3 people.
  - **Paddleboard**
    - $35.00 - $70.00 - Two paddleboard experiences to choose from.
  - **Kayak**
    - $30.00 - $60.00 - Singles & Tandems. Sit-in & Sit-on Top Styles available.
- **Activities**: Glass bottom boat tours, paddling, safari train tour (free), mini zoo, wildlife viewing, birdwatching, museum

See Florida's Wild Heart Through Glass-Bottom Boats

One of America's largest and most iconic springs, Silver Springs has long been a must-visit destination for nature lovers and history enthusiasts alike. Best known for its world-famous glass-bottom boat tours, this park offers a rare glimpse into an underwater world, where crystal-clear waters reveal submerged caves, ancient artifacts, vibrant aquatic life, and even movie props from Hollywood classics filmed here decades ago.

Beyond the springs, the park's serene gardens and historic structures reflect its rich past. In the late 1800s, Silver Springs was one of Florida's premier destinations, drawing visitors from across the country—many of whom arrived by steamship, eager to experience the magic of these pristine waters. Today, the park still exudes old Florida charm, inviting guests to explore its scenic walking paths, shaded picnic areas, and tranquil natural surroundings.

For those looking to venture beyond the boat tour, Silver Springs offers kayaking, canoeing, hiking, and abundant wildlife viewing. Keep an eye out for manatees, turtles, wading birds, and even wild monkeys that inhabit the area.

Whether you're floating over the springs in a glass-bottom boat, paddling through the winding waterways, or simply enjoying the peaceful atmosphere, Silver Springs is a place where nature and history come together to create an unforgettable Florida experience.

Hours	8 a.m. to sundown 365 days a year
Phone	352.261.5840
Location	5656 E Silver Springs Blvd, Silver Springs, FL 34488
Website	silversprings.com

Suggested Supplies

Water (only non-disposable containers)	Snacks (food is available)	Sunscreen
Stroller or wagon for kids	Bug repellant	Backpack or sling bag
Bug repellant	Binoculars	

Jacksonville

Jacksonville is a gateway to adventure, a city where history, nature, and culture come together in a way that few places can match. While many know Jacksonville for its beaches, lively riverfront, and urban attractions, there's an entire world of hidden gems and off-the-beaten-path destinations just a short drive away.

Within an hour's journey, you can walk among the ruins of historic plantations, explore untouched barrier islands, paddle through crystal-clear springs, or discover centuries-old forts that tell the stories of Florida's past. Whether you're looking for a peaceful nature escape, a deep dive into history, or a charming small-town getaway, this region offers a diverse mix of experiences that feel far removed from the city's fast pace.

From the mystical landscapes of Big Talbot Island's Boneyard Beach to the wild horses of Cumberland Island, this section highlights the best day trips and hidden retreats around Jacksonville. So pack a picnic, grab your binoculars, and get ready to explore the side of Northeast Florida that many overlook—but few forget.

Jacksonville, Florida

Total day trip time: approximately 5 hours. 40-minute drive round trip (multiple entrances, so drive time may vary), leaving 4+ hours for hiking, biking, history, and wildlife viewing.

Dogs: Yes (Dogs are allowed on trails and on the grounds at the Preserve (including Fort Caroline, Kingsley Plantation, Theodore Roosevelt Area, and Cedar Point), leashed, no longer than 6'. Only service animals are allowed inside the visitor centers, historic structures, or other NPS structures.

- **Fees:**
  - Tumucuan Ecological and Historic Preserve: $0
  - Ribault Club: $0
  - Camp Milton: $0
- **Activities**: History, hiking, biking, paddling, wildlife viewing, birdwatching

Where Salt Marshes, Ancient Trails, and Florida's Earliest Stories Meet

Just outside Jacksonville lies one of Florida's most fascinating and diverse landscapes, where untamed wilderness and deep-rooted history converge. The Timucuan Ecological and Historic Preserve spans salt marshes, hardwood forests, and ancient shell mounds, preserving the stories of Native Americans, European settlers, enslaved people, and plantation owners who left their mark on this land.

There is so much to do here that I couldn't possibly cover it all in one book, so I'll focus on the areas managed by the National Park Service (NPS)—some of the most historically and naturally significant places in the preserve. Whether you love hiking under towering oaks, biking through pine forests, paddling through winding salt marshes, or simply soaking in the sights and sounds of Florida's wild beauty, you'll find it all here. And if history is what draws you in, the **self-guided audio walking tours at Fort Caroline, Cedar Point, and Kingsley Plantation** make it easy to experience the past at your own pace.

Whether you come for the history, the hiking, the paddling, or the wildlife, the Timucuan Preserve offers an experience unlike anywhere else in Florida. This is a place where the past is never far from the present, where the landscape itself tells the stories of those who came before. If you want to truly appreciate the wild beauty and deep history of Florida, there's no better place to start.

Stepping Into Florida's Complex History

Kingsley Plantation is the perfect place to begin exploring the preserve. The oldest standing plantation house in Florida, this site tells a complex and often difficult story of wealth, enslavement, and resilience. Zephaniah Kingsley and his wife, Anna Kingsley—once an enslaved woman who later became a landowner herself—ran this plantation on Fort George Island in the early 1800s. Today, visitors can walk through the rows of tabby slave cabins, explore the 18th-century plantation home, and hear the voices of the past through the self-guided audio tour, which brings this history to life. The grounds are open daily, though the main house is only open on weekends.

Further south, **Fort Caroline National Memorial** marks the site of the first French settlement in North America, established in 1564. While the original fort is long gone, a faithful reconstruction now stands, allowing visitors to imagine the struggles of the French settlers who attempted to carve out a home here, only to be wiped out by the Spanish in a violent takeover. The audio tour guides visitors through the fort's turbulent past, and nearby trails wind through dense maritime forests and lead to scenic overlooks, where you can see the same waterways that made this land so valuable—and so vulnerable.

Outdoor Adventures in the Preserve

For those looking to explore the natural side of the preserve, **Cedar Point** is one of the best places to start. With miles of trails winding through maritime hammocks, salt marsh, and pine flatwoods, it's a peaceful place for hiking, wildlife watching, and bicycling. Bicycles are allowed on the trails here, making it one of the best spots in the preserve to explore on two wheels. Keep an eye out for wading birds, dolphins, and even manatees in the waterways that weave through the landscape.

For a more rugged experience, the **Theodore Roosevelt Area** offers a wild and secluded retreat into Florida's past. Once owned by conservationist Willie Browne, this land remains largely untouched, with trails winding through towering oak trees and pine forests. Most trails here are hiking only, though bicycles are allowed on the Blue Trail (Willie Browne Trail). This area feels like stepping into Old Florida, offering an escape from the modern world into a landscape that has remained unchanged for centuries.

While bicycling is a great way to explore the preserve, there are some restrictions. Bikes are not allowed on the trails or grounds at Fort Caroline National Memorial and Kingsley Plantation to preserve the historic integrity of these sites. Likewise, in the Theodore Roosevelt Area, bicycles are only allowed on the Blue Trail, but they are permitted throughout Cedar Point.

Exploring the Preserve by Water

While the trails offer a great way to explore on foot or by bike, paddling through the salt marshes might just be the best way to experience this landscape. With two-thirds of the preserve made up of these winding creeks and estuaries, it's a haven for ospreys, herons, manatees, and even the occasional dolphin. There's something incredibly peaceful about gliding through these untouched waters, where the only sounds are the rustling of the marsh grass and the occasional call of a shorebird.

Explore Fort George Island with the **Virtual Ranger Driving Tour**

For those looking to experience the history, landscapes, and wildlife of Fort George Island, the Virtual Ranger Tour of the Saturiwa Trail offers a self-guided driving experience like no other. This scenic 4.4-mile loop begins at the historic Ribault Club, winding through oak-canopied roads, past historic sites, and alongside breathtaking coastal vistas.

This tour isn't just about history—it's a journey through architecture, natural habitats, and ever-changing seasonal beauty. Depending on when you visit, you'll get a completely different experience. Spring brings vibrant wildflowers and flickering fireflies, summer offers lush greenery and peak colors, fall provides the quietest and least crowded drives, while winter's cool air is perfect for rolling down the windows and enjoying the ride.

All you need to embark on this Old Florida adventure is a car CD player or a mobile internet device, allowing you to follow along with narrated stories of the Timucua people, early European explorers, and the island's transformation over the centuries. The audio tour provides rich details about the island's architecture, historic structures, and ecological significance, giving visitors a deeper appreciation for this untouched slice of Florida's past.

Wildlife is everywhere on Fort George Island, so drive with caution. Gopher tortoise crossings are marked in high-traffic wildlife areas, and it's not uncommon to see deer, birds of prey, and other native animals along the way.

To access the Virtual Ranger Tour on your phone, follow the instructions provided below and get ready to explore one of Florida's most unique and historic landscapes at your own pace.

An Historic Must-Visit for Civil War Buffs

For Civil War buffs and history lovers alike, Camp Milton Historic Preserve offers a rare chance to step back in time and experience one of Florida's most significant Civil War sites. Once a strategic Confederate encampment, this location served as a defensive stronghold along the Baldwin rail line in 1864, housing thousands of troops. Today, it stands as one of the most well-preserved Civil War sites in the state, offering visitors a unique blend of history, education, and scenic beauty.

At the heart of the preserve is a state-of-the-art educational center, where Civil War artifacts and interactive exhibits bring the era to life. A wooden boardwalk leads to preserved earthworks, allowing visitors to see the very fortifications that once protected this critical supply route. A highlight of the site is McGirts Creek Bridge, a replica of a campaign bridge, showcasing the ingenuity of military engineering during the war.

Beyond its military history, Camp Milton also offers a glimpse into Florida's rural past. An authentic 1800s farmstead provides a look at everyday life during the Civil War era, from farming techniques to the daily struggles of early settlers. Whether you're walking the historic trails, exploring the earthworks, or delving into the artifacts at the visitor center, Camp Milton Historic Preserve is a must-visit destination for anyone fascinated by the Civil War and Florida's role in it.

At Timucuan, history isn't confined to books or museum exhibits—it's woven into the land itself, waiting to be explored one trail, one paddle, and one story at a time.

Audio Tour

Simply use your phone's camera to scan the QR code, then follow the link that appears. The tour is divided into individual audio segments, allowing you to listen at your own pace as you reach each designated stop along the route.

Hours	<ul><li>Timucuan Preserve Visitor Center (Fort Caroline) and Kingsley Plantation Visitor Contact Station<ul><li>9:00 am to 4:30 PM, Wednesday through Sunday</li><li>Closed Monday & Tuesday</li><li>Closed Thanksgiving Day, Christmas Day, and New Year's Day.</li></ul></li><li>Fort Caroline grounds<ul><li>grounds gates are locked at 5:00 pm</li></ul></li><li>Kingsley Plantation<ul><li>grounds gates are locked at 5:00 pm</li></ul></li><li>Camp Milton: 9 a.m. to 5: p.m. daily</li><li>Theodore Roosevelt Area: sunrise to sunset</li><li>Cedar Point: sunrise to sunset</li></ul>
Phone	**Fort Caroline:**904-641-7155 **Theodore Roosevelt Area:** 904-641-7155 **Kingsley Plantation:** 904-251-353 **Cedar Point:** 904-641-7155 **Camp Milton** 904-630-2489
Location (Each area has a different address)	**Fort Caroline:** 12713 Fort Caroline Road Jacksonville, FL 32225 **Theodore Roosevelt Area:** 13175 Mt. Pleasant Road Jacksonville, Florida 32225 **Kingsley Plantation:** 11676 Palmetto Avenue Jacksonville, Florida 32226

	Camp Milton: 1175 Halsema Rd N. Jacksonville, FL 32220 **Cedar Point:** 9023 Cedar Point Road Jacksonville, Florida 32218
Website	nps.gov/timu/

Suggested Supplies

Note: There are no concessions anywhere in the preserve. However, the preserve is just outside an urban area where food is available.

Water	Picnic food	Picnic supplies
Picnic blanket (Picnic tables and shelters are available at Fort Caroline, Kingsley Plantation, Cedar Point, and the Theodore Roosevelt Area.)		
Backpack or sling bag (if hiking or biking)	Sunscreen	Bug repellant
Stroller or wagon for children	Waterproof bags (if paddling)	Snacks

St. George Island rentals:

Jolly Roger: They have everything you could think of, from bicycles and kayaks to child bike tagalongs and gas grills, plus everything for fishing. jollyrogersgi.com Email:JollyRogerBeachShop@gmail.com

Phone:

- Shop: (850) 927-2999
- Secondary Phone: 850-927-4004

Hours: 9a.m. to 7p.m. Seasonally – Call or email for current hours.

Island Adventures: Bikes, child trailer, fishing carts, chairs, and umbrellas. sgiadventures.com

Phone: 850-927-3655

Email: info@SGIAdventures.com.

VayK Gear: Bikes, boards, kayaks, beach games, beach chairs and accessories. vaykgear.com/st-george-island

Email: support@vaykgear.com

Hours: Monday – Sunday 9a.m. to 5p.m.

Jacksonville, Florida

Total day trip time: approximately 3 hours. 45-minute drive round trip, leaving 3 ¼ hours to get to know the big cats.

Dogs: No

- **Day Tours**
  - Adults: $15
  - Children (3-11): $7
  - Children (2 and younger): Always free and do not require a ticket
- **Night Feeding**
  - Adults: $35 for a general admission ticket ($45 – package deal ticket, which includes free t-shirt ($24 value) and free drink or snow cone)
  - Children (3-11): $20 general admission ticket
  - Children (2 and younger): Always free and do not require a ticket
- **Enrichment Tour**
  - Adults: $15
  - Children (3-11): $7
  - Children (2 and younger): Always free and do not require a ticket
- **Activities**: Animal viewing/encounters

A Wild Encounter with Big Cats and More

For those who have ever dreamed of getting up close to tigers, lions, cougars, leopards, and other majestic big cats, Catty Shack Ranch Wildlife Sanctuary offers an unforgettable experience just outside of Jacksonville. As a nonprofit rescue and lifelong care facility, Catty Shack Ranch provides a safe and loving forever home for exotic animals that cannot survive in the wild. Whether you visit during the day, at night for an exhilarating feeding tour, or take part in an Enrichment Tour, every visit to Catty Shack Ranch is an opportunity to witness the incredible power, intelligence, and personalities of these amazing creatures.

Daytime Tours: Meet the Residents at Your Own Pace

Your visit begins with a short introductory video, offering insight into the sanctuary's mission, history, and dedication to conservation. From there, you'll embark on a self-guided walking tour, where you can observe tigers, lions, leopards, bobcats, cougars, servals, caracals, foxes, coatimundis, and even bears in their naturalistic habitats. Unlike traditional zoos, this experience allows for a closer, more personal connection to the animals.

Along the way, knowledgeable volunteers and staff members are stationed throughout the grounds, ready to answer questions and share the stories of each rescued resident. Most visitors take 45 minutes to an hour to explore the sanctuary, but you're welcome to take your time, revisit your favorite animals, and simply enjoy the peaceful surroundings. A concession stand offers snacks and drinks, while a gift shop provides souvenirs, with proceeds directly benefiting the animals. Photography is encouraged, so don't forget your camera!

The facility is wheelchair and stroller-accessible, with packed dirt and grass pathways that make navigation easy. Last admittance for daytime tours is 3:00 PM, ensuring all visitors have time to fully enjoy the experience.

The Enrichment Tour: A Behind-the-Scenes Look at Animal Care

For those seeking a deeper understanding of animal welfare, the Enrichment Tour is a must-do. Enrichment is an essential part of caring for big cats and other exotic animals, providing mental stimulation, physical exercise, and opportunities for them to engage in natural behaviors. This tour highlights the many ways that keepers create science-based enrichment programs, similar to those developed in accredited zoos and wildlife centers.

Enrichment can include puzzle feeders, scent trails, interactive toys, and even training exercises designed to give the animals choices, challenges, and control over their environment. By participating in this tour, visitors can see firsthand how these majestic predators play, problem-solve, and interact with their surroundings, keeping them engaged and active.

Night Feedings: See the Big Cats Come to Life

For a truly thrilling experience, Catty Shack Ranch's Night Feeding events, held every Friday and Saturday from 6:00 to 7:30 PM, offer a rare look at the sanctuary's residents in action. As dusk settles, the big cats become more vocal and energetic, eagerly anticipating their evening meal.

The experience begins with a self-guided walking tour, where you can observe the animals as they prepare for feeding time. At 7:00 PM, the real excitement begins. Executive Director Curt LoGiudice leads visitors through the sanctuary, stopping at each habitat to provide fascinating facts about the species, their history, and their care. As you watch tigers and lions devour more than 600 pounds of beef and chicken—bones and all—you'll gain a new appreciation for these powerful predators.

Since Night Feedings often sell out, it's recommended to reserve tickets online in advance. Before leaving, be sure to stop by the gift shop and even consider "adopting" one of the animals, which helps support their lifelong care.

A Unique and Meaningful Wildlife Experience

Whether you come during the day for a leisurely tour, in the evening for the excitement of a feeding, or for an in-depth look at animal enrichment, Catty Shack Ranch offers a one-of-a-kind experience for animal lovers of all ages. More than just a wildlife attraction, this sanctuary is a place of compassion, education, and conservation, giving rescued big cats and exotic animals a safe and loving forever home.

Hours	Day Tours 1:00 – 3:00 p.m. Enrichment Tours are offered every Sunday 1:00 – 3:00 p.m. Night Feedings are held every Friday & Saturday 6:00 – 7:30 p.m., Last Admittance at 7:00 p.m.
Phone	904-757-3603
Location	1860 Starratt Road Jacksonville, FL 32226
Website	cattyshack.org

Suggested Supplies

Stroller or wagon for kids	Bug repellant	Close-toed shoes
Water	Sunscreen	Binoculars

Jacksonville, Florida

Total day trip time: approximately 5 hours. 1-hour round-trip drive, leaving 4 hours for fun and exploring.

Dogs: Yes (Not allowed on beaches, playgrounds, or in buildings)

- **Fees:**
  o $2.00 per person to access the George Crady Bridge Fishing Pier.
  o $3.00 per vehicle entrance fee to access the Bluffs picnic area, Blackrock trailhead and Big Pine trailhead.
  o $4.00 launch fee for each boat/trailer.
- **Activities:** Hiking, wildlife viewing, fishing, boating, birdwatching

From Boneyard Beach to Hidden Trails

Perched along Florida's northeast coast, Big Talbot Island State Park is a place where untouched beaches, towering live oaks, and dramatic coastal landscapes create one of the most unique outdoor experiences in the state. Unlike the bustling beaches of Florida's tourist hubs, Big Talbot Island remains a wild and serene retreat, perfect for those looking to explore, relax, and connect with nature.

One of the park's most iconic and otherworldly sights is Boneyard Beach, where centuries-old live oaks and cedar trees—bleached and smoothed by sun and salt—lie scattered along the shore like driftwood sculptures. The result is a stunning, almost surreal landscape that draws photographers, artists, and nature lovers alike. It's a place to walk along the water's edge, admire the contrast between the white skeleton trees and black rock formations, and watch the waves roll in.

Beyond its striking shoreline, Big Talbot Island is a paradise for paddlers and hikers. Kayaking through the salt marshes of Simpson Creek offers a completely different view of the island, with the chance to spot dolphins, wading birds, and even the occasional manatee. The Blackrock Trail is a must for those looking to explore on foot, leading visitors through twisting live oaks, palmetto groves, and down to the beach, where the unique black rock formations resemble a lunar landscape.

For birdwatchers, the park is a haven. As part of the Great Florida Birding and Wildlife Trail, Big Talbot Island is home to herons, egrets, wood storks, and even bald eagles. The bluffs overlooking the salt marshes provide some of the best birdwatching spots in the region, offering a chance to observe these magnificent creatures in their natural habitat.

Cyclists and casual walkers will enjoy the Timucuan Trail, a paved multi-use path that winds through Big Talbot and neighboring Little Talbot Island, offering an easy and scenic way to take in the lush maritime forest and coastal views. Picnic areas tucked beneath moss-draped oaks provide the perfect spot to unwind and enjoy a meal surrounded by nature.

Whether you're paddling through quiet marshes, walking among ancient driftwood giants, or simply soaking in the peaceful surroundings, Big Talbot Island State Park offers a rare glimpse of Florida's coastline as it once was—wild, rugged, and breathtakingly beautiful.

Hours	8 a.m. until sundown, 365 days a year.
Phone	904-251-2320
Location	15500 Bucaneer Trail, Jacksonville, Fl 32226
Website	floridastateparks.org/parks-and-trails/big-talbot-island-state-park

Suggested Supplies

Water	Snacks/picnic supplies	Bug repellant
Binoculars	Stroller or wagon for kids	Close-toed shoes or hiking boots
Water shoes	Sunscreen	Towles/beach blanket

Jacksonville, Florida

Total day trip time: approximately 6 hours. 1-hour round-trip drive, leaving 5 hours for wet-and-wild fun.

Dogs: No

- **Fees:**
  - Ticket prices vary depending on activities/specials, typically beginning around $40.00 per person.
- **Activities:** swimming, floating, water slides, games

Water Slides, Wave Pools, and Family Fun Await

For families, thrill-seekers, and anyone looking for a fun and action-packed day, Adventure Landing & Shipwreck Island Water Park in Jacksonville Beach delivers non-stop excitement with something for everyone. Whether you're racing go-karts, plunging down water slides, or testing your skills in the arcade, this lively entertainment park offers a perfect mix of adventure and relaxation.

The day kicks off with a splash at Shipwreck Island Water Park, where the wave pool mimics the rolling ocean, letting guests bob and ride the waves without the sand. Those looking for a more relaxing experience can float along the lazy river, while adrenaline junkies take on the high-speed water slides, twisting and turning through tunnels before splashing into the pools below. Younger guests will love the interactive kiddie play area, designed with smaller slides, water cannons, and plenty of opportunities to cool off.

Once everyone has dried off, the fun continues on land. The miniature golf course, designed with creative obstacles and fun themes, is a great way to challenge friends and family. Over at the go-kart track, the competition heats up as drivers race around curves and straightaways in a battle for first place.

For those who love gaming, the mega arcade is packed with classic and modern video games, redemption games, and prizes to win. Whether it's a friendly game of air hockey or mastering the claw machines, the arcade offers hours of entertainment. Right next door, the laser tag arena provides an interactive adventure, where players strategize and dodge laser beams in a fast-paced competition.

Kids can take a turn at the batting cages, hop on the Wacky Worm Rollercoaster, or enjoy the gentle bouncing fun of the Frog Hopper ride. For animal lovers, Gator Alley gives visitors a chance to observe and even feed real alligators in a safe environment. And before the day ends, stopping by the Sweet Adventures Candy Shop is a must, offering a variety of sweet treats and snacks to satisfy any craving.

From high-energy thrills to laid-back fun, Adventure Landing & Shipwreck Island Water Park is a destination packed with activities that make for an unforgettable day trip. Whether you're sliding, racing, or gaming, there's no shortage of excitement waiting to be discovered.

Hours	**Hours vary** by month/day/activity (between 10 a.m./noon opening to 3 p.m./10 p.m. closing) Check the website calendar.
Phone	904-246-4386
Location	1944 Beach Blvd (U.S. 90) Jacksonville Beach, FL 32250
Website	jacksonville-beach.adventurelanding.com/

Suggested Supplies

Sunscreen	Water shoes	Water (no outside food allowed. Water must be in clear bottles)
Stroller or wagon for the kids	Towels	Change of clothes
Sunglasses	Bug repellant	

Jacksonville, Florida

Total day trip time: approximately 5 hours. 1-hour round-trip drive, leaving 4 hours for sun and fun.

Dogs: Yes

- **Fees:**
  - $3.00 for Pedestrians and Bicycles
  - $5.00 for Vehicles up to 6 people ($1 for each additional person
- **Activities:** Beach, biking, hiking, paddling, fishing, birdwatching.

A Coastal Escape for Adventure and Relaxation

Nestled along the Atlantic coast, Kathryn Abbey Hanna Park offers 450 acres of outdoor adventure, scenic beauty, and serene relaxation, making it one of Jacksonville's best-kept secrets. Whether you're looking for a peaceful day on the beach, an exhilarating bike ride through the woods, or a quiet moment by the water, this park truly has something for everyone.

A Perfect Day by the Water

With miles of pristine beachfront, Hanna Park is the perfect spot to sink your toes into the sand, listen to the waves, and enjoy the coastal breeze. Swimmers, surfers, and sunbathers all flock to the wide, uncrowded shoreline, where the Atlantic's rolling waves provide the perfect playground for water lovers. Those looking for a quieter aquatic experience can head inland to the park's freshwater pond, ideal for canoeing, kayaking, and fishing.

During the summer, families with young children can cool off at the splash park, where kids can play under fountains and water sprayers. For those planning a gathering or picnic, the park offers pavilions available for rental, making it easy to set up a home base for the day.

Scenic Trails for Every Explorer

Hanna Park is a hiker and cyclist's dream, with over 20 miles of scenic trails winding through dense coastal hammocks, towering oaks, and along stunning shorelines. The off-road mountain biking trails are especially popular, offering a variety of experiences for all skill levels. Beginners and families can enjoy the wide, flat, easy trails, while experienced riders can challenge themselves on the steep, single-track paths with log crossings and tight turns.

For those who prefer a slower pace, the park's hiking trails offer a peaceful escape into nature, where the sounds of birdsong and rustling leaves replace the noise of the city. Along the way, keep an eye out for shorebirds, wading birds, foxes, and even the occasional alligator.

A Haven for Wildlife

Hanna Park is teeming with wildlife, making it a great destination for birdwatchers and nature enthusiasts. From shorebirds darting along the sand to great blue herons standing tall in the marsh, the park offers a glimpse into Florida's diverse coastal ecosystem. Between May and October, the beach becomes even more special as it transforms into a protected nesting site for sea turtles, an awe-inspiring sight for lucky visitors.

A Coastal Retreat for Every Kind of Adventurer

Whether you're here for a leisurely beach day, an adrenaline-pumping mountain bike ride, a quiet paddle on the pond, or a peaceful nature walk, Kathryn Abbey Hanna Park is the kind of place that keeps visitors coming back. With unspoiled beauty, endless recreation, and a true connection to nature, it's the perfect escape just minutes from the city, yet a world away.

Hours	**Open daily**
	• 8:00 a.m. - 8:00 p.m. during Daylight Savings Time
	• 8:00 a.m. - 6:00 p.m. during Eastern Standard Time
Phone	904-255-6767
Location	500 Wonderwood Dr Jacksonville, FL 32233
Website	timucuanparks.org/parks/kathryn-abbey-hanna-park/

Suggested Supplies

Sunscreen	Bug repellant	Sunglasses
Towels	Blanket or chairs for the beach	Water
Snacks	Picnic pack	Water shoes
Hiking boots or walking shoes	Waste bags for Fido	Binoculars

Jacksonville, Florida

Total day trip time: approximately 5 hours. 1-hour round-trip drive, leaving 4 for fun and exploring.

Dogs: Yes

- **Fees:**
  - $0
- **Activities:** Walking/hiking, biking, paddling, birdwatching, wildlife viewing

A Hidden Paradise of Marshes, Trails, and Tranquility Awaits

Tucked away in Jacksonville's unspoiled coastal wilderness, Seven Creeks Recreation Area is a nature lover's paradise, offering over 30 miles of scenic trails, winding waterways, and peaceful landscapes that invite exploration. This unique network of parks and preserves is where freshwater meets saltwater, creating a diverse habitat for wildlife and a stunning backdrop for outdoor adventures.

With seven different creeks weaving through the area, this is one of the best places in North Florida for kayaking and canoeing. Paddlers can glide through serene tidal marshes, cypress-lined waterways, and open estuaries, often spotting dolphins, manatees, ospreys, and great blue herons along the way. The slow-moving creeks make it an ideal destination for both beginner and experienced kayakers looking for a peaceful escape into nature.

For those who prefer to stay on land, hiking and biking trails wind through a variety of landscapes, from oak hammocks and pine forests to salt marshes and riverbanks. The trails range from easy strolls to longer, more immersive treks, offering opportunities to see deer, wild turkeys, and even the occasional bobcat. Birdwatchers will be in paradise, as the area is home to an incredible variety of wading birds, songbirds, and birds of prey.

One of the highlights of Seven Creeks Recreation Area is its sense of solitude. With fewer crowds than other Jacksonville parks, visitors can truly connect with nature, take in the peaceful sounds of the marsh, and enjoy the beauty of an untouched Florida landscape. Whether you're looking for a quiet morning paddle, a challenging hike, a scenic picnic spot, or simply a place to breathe in the fresh coastal air, Seven Creeks Recreation Area is a hidden gem just waiting to be explored.

Hours	Daily 8 a.m. until sundown
Phone	904-374-1107
Location	5500 Cedar Point Road Jacksonville, FL 32226
Website	timucuanparks.org/7-creeks-jax/

Suggested Supplies

Sunscreen	Bug repellant	Water
Snacks	Walking shoes/hiking boots	Stroller or wagon for children
Binoculars	Picnic pack	Waste bags for Fido
Sunglasses	Water shoes or old sneakers (boating)	

Folkston, Georgia

Total day trip time: approximately 6 ½ hours. 2 ¼-hour drive round trip, leaving 4 hours for fun and exploring.

Dogs: Yes Dogs are allowed **in limited areas** of Okefenokee National Wildlife Refuge.

- **Fees:**
  - $5.00 per car
  - **Free Days**
    - January 20, 2025 (Martin Luther King, Jr. Day)
    - June 19, 2025 (Juneteenth)
    - September 27, 2025 (National Public Lands Day)
    - October 12, 2025 (First Sunday of National Wildlife Refuge Week)
    - November 11, 2025 (Veteran's Day)
- **Activities:** Wildlife viewing drive, hiking, canoe/kayaking.

A Land of Mystery and Beauty—Where Alligators Glide and Spanish Moss Sways

Stepping into the Okefenokee National Wildlife Refuge is like stepping into another world—one of mysterious blackwater swamps, winding waterways, towering cypress trees, and an astonishing array of wildlife. Covering over 400,000 acres across Georgia and Florida, this vast and untamed wilderness is one of the largest intact freshwater ecosystems in North America and a haven for both nature lovers and adventure seekers.

The Suwannee Canal Recreation Area (Main Entrance)

With so much to explore, the refuge offers something for everyone. Paddlers can glide silently through the dark, mirror-like waters, where cypress trees draped in Spanish moss cast eerie reflections and alligators bask along the banks. Canoeing and kayaking are among the most immersive ways to experience the Okefenokee, allowing visitors to navigate the endless maze of channels and prairies, often spotting turtles, wading birds, otters, and even sandhill cranes along the way.

For those who prefer to stay on dry land, boardwalks and scenic trails wind through the refuge, offering up-close views of rare plants, wildflowers, and a thriving population of native wildlife. The Swamp Island Drive, a 7.5-mile scenic route, provides breathtaking views of the wetlands, with stops along the way for short hikes, wildlife viewing platforms, and interpretive exhibits.

Wildlife enthusiasts will find no shortage of opportunities to observe the incredible biodiversity that thrives in this ancient wetland. The refuge is home to more than 200 species of birds, black bears, white-tailed deer, and the famous Okefenokee alligators, which can often be seen sunning themselves along the edges of the water. Boat tours offer an effortless way to take in the beauty of the swamp, with local guides providing insight into the refuge's history, ecology, and folklore.

As the sun sets over the swamp, the sounds of tree frogs, barred owls, and distant alligator calls create an atmosphere unlike any other in Florida. Whether you're paddling through the channels, walking the trails, or simply taking in the quiet majesty of the landscape, Okefenokee National Wildlife Refuge is a place where nature still reigns supreme—an unforgettable experience for those who seek the wild beauty of the South.

Okefenokee Adventures offers guided boat tours, canoe/kayak rentals, boat rentals, and a gift shop to visitors. Okefenokee Adventures also provides food service on-site and is a great place to stop in and pick up any last-minute items for your trip in the swamp and check out the most recent wildlife sightings.

Hours	March 1 to October 31: half an hour before sunrise to 7:30 p.m. November 1 to the end of February: half an hour before sunrise to 5:30 p.m..
Phone	912-496-7836
Location	2700 Suwannee Canal Road, Folkston, GA 31537
Website	fws.gov/refuge/okefenokee

Suggested Supplies

Water	Snacks	Bug repellant
Close-toed shoes	Stroller or wagon for children	Sunscreen
Picnic supplies if bringing a meal	Binoculars	Long sleeve shirt/long pants (biting flies can be vicious)

Orlando

When most people think of Orlando, their minds immediately go to theme parks, roller coasters, and bustling tourist attractions. But beyond the towering castles and adrenaline-pumping rides, Orlando offers a whole world of outdoor adventures, scenic escapes, and hidden gems that many visitors—and even locals—overlook.

Surrounded by lakes, rivers, forests, and vast conservation areas, Orlando is a paradise for outdoor lovers. Whether you want to paddle through cypress-lined springs, hike along shaded trails, zip through the treetops, or take in the city skyline from a 400-foot observation wheel, there's something for everyone. From the serene beauty of Harry P. Leu Gardens to the wild encounters at Gatorland, Orlando is full of unexpected adventures that go far beyond the theme parks.

Whether you're seeking solitude in nature, an exciting outdoor challenge, or a peaceful escape from the crowds, these destinations offer a different side of Orlando—one that's just waiting to be explored.

Orlando, Florida

Total day trip time: approximately 4 ½ hours. 30-minute drive round trip, leaving 4 hours for garden viewing, picnicking, birdwatching.
Dogs: No (only ADA approved service dogs allowed)
- **Fees:**
    o $15.00 Adult
    o $10.00 Child (4-17 years old)
    o $0 Members, Child under 4, Active-duty Military
- **Activities**: walking, unique horticulture viewing, birdwatching, historical home tour, picnicking

A Tranquil Escape in the Heart of Orlando

Just minutes from the bustling theme parks and busy city streets, Harry P. Leu Gardens offers a peaceful retreat into nature, where visitors can wander through 50 acres of lush gardens, shaded pathways, and scenic lakes. A true hidden gem in Orlando, this beautifully maintained botanical paradise invites guests to slow down, breathe in the fresh air, and immerse themselves in a world of blooming flowers, towering oaks, and tropical greenery.

Walking through Leu Gardens is like stepping into a living work of art. The winding trails lead visitors past vibrant flower beds, tranquil ponds, and meticulously curated plant collections that showcase the best of Florida's natural beauty. Seasonal displays ensure that no two visits are exactly the same, with ever-changing bursts of roses, camellias, azaleas, and orchids filling the landscape with color and fragrance.

For those who appreciate the unusual and exotic, the gardens also feature palms, bamboo, and a sprawling tropical rainforest that transports visitors to a lush, jungle-like setting. The butterfly garden is a particular favorite, where visitors can watch delicate, colorful butterflies flutter among nectar-rich flowers.

Beyond the natural beauty, Leu Gardens is also home to the historic Leu House Museum, a restored 19th-century estate that tells the story of Harry P. Leu and his family, who gifted the gardens to the city of Orlando. The guided tours of the home offer a glimpse into Florida's past, showcasing antique furnishings, architectural details, and the lifestyle of a wealthy Florida family in the early 1900s.

Visitors can explore at their own pace or join a guided tour to gain deeper insight into the diverse plant life and the history of the gardens. Throughout the year, seasonal events and educational programs offer unique experiences, from gardening workshops and botanical lectures to outdoor movie nights and plant sales. The gardens are also a paradise for photographers and birdwatchers, with breathtaking landscapes and an abundance of native wildlife.

For those looking to simply relax, there are plenty of quiet spots to sit and take in the surroundings, and while food isn't sold on-site, guests are welcome to bring a picnic and enjoy a peaceful meal among the flowers.

For those seeking a peaceful escape from the fast pace of Orlando's attractions, Harry P. Leu Gardens offers a refreshing change of scenery. Whether you're a nature lover, history enthusiast, photographer, or simply looking for a quiet place to unwind, this hidden oasis provides a perfect setting to relax and reconnect with nature.

Hours	*March – September*
	    9 a.m. – 6 p.m. daily
	    The last entry is one hour before closing time
	    9 a.m. – 8 p.m. – Late Night Thursdays
	    The last entry is one hour before closing time
	September - November
	    9 a.m. – 5 p.m. daily
	    The last entry is one hour before closing time
	December - January
	    9 a.m. – 4 p.m. daily
	    The last entry is one hour before closing time
	Historic Leu House Museum
	    The Historic Leu House Museum is open Tuesday – Sunday from 10 a.m. – 1 p.m. for guided tours. The Historic Leu House Museum is **closed in July**. Hours are subject to change due to events.

Phone	407-246-2620
Location	1920 North Forest Avenue Orlando, Florida 32803
Website	leugardens.org

Suggested Supplies

Water	Picnic supplies	Bug repellant
Sunscreen	Binoculars	walking shoes
Stroller or wagon for children	Wheelchairs available free on-site (first come, first served)	Snacks/picnic food
Blanket (picnic)	Wipes (when just a napkin won't do)	Backpack or picnic basket

Orlando, Florida

Total day trip time: approximately 3 ½ to 5 ½ hours. 30-minute round-trip drive, leaving 3-5 hours for rides and excitement.
Dogs: No
- **Fees:**
  - Ticket prices start at $33.00 for adults and $25.00 for ages 2-12.
    - Package tickets available for the Eye, Madame Tussauds Orlando and SEA LIFE Orlando Aquarium.
- **Activities**: 400-foot Ferris wheel and other rides, Aquarium and unique museums.

A Bird's-Eye View of the City's Skyline

Rising 400 feet above International Drive, The Orlando Eye, now known as The Wheel at ICON Park, offers breathtaking, panoramic views of Orlando and beyond. This iconic observation wheel, one of the tallest on the East Coast, provides a smooth, slow-moving ride inside a spacious, air-conditioned capsule, allowing guests to take in unforgettable sights of theme parks, shimmering lakes, and even the Kennedy Space Center on a clear day. Whether you're visiting during the day for a bright, sunlit view of the city or at night when Orlando glows with dazzling lights, The Wheel is an experience that changes with every visit.

Each ride lasts about 20 minutes, giving visitors plenty of time to soak in the 360-degree views. The floor-to-ceiling glass windows in each capsule offer unobstructed scenery, while an interactive tablet display inside provides information on what you're looking at. From up high, you can see Walt Disney World, Universal Orlando, downtown Orlando's skyline, and even Cape Canaveral in the distance.

For a special experience, visitors can upgrade to a Sky Bar capsule, where they can enjoy a glass of champagne or beer while taking in the views. Whether you're celebrating a special occasion or just looking for a peaceful retreat from the crowds, The Wheel provides a serene, memorable moment high above the city.

The Orlando Eye is just one part of the larger ICON Park entertainment complex, where visitors can enjoy a variety of attractions, restaurants, and shops. Ticket packages often include other must-see experiences, allowing guests to bundle multiple attractions for one price.

Sea Life Orlando Aquarium – Explore a stunning underwater world, where you can walk through a 360-degree ocean tunnel surrounded by sharks, sea turtles, and colorful fish.

Madame Tussauds Orlando – Pose alongside lifelike wax figures of celebrities, superheroes, and historical icons, making for a fun and interactive experience.

Museum of Illusions – Step into a world of mind-bending exhibits and optical illusions, where things aren't always as they seem.

7D Dark Ride Adventure – An action-packed, interactive gaming experience, where guests battle zombies, robots, and more in an immersive motion ride.

Whether you're looking for a romantic date night, a fun-filled family outing, or a relaxing break from the theme parks, The Wheel at ICON Park offers a unique and unforgettable perspective of Orlando. With its stunning views, relaxing ride, and the exciting attractions nearby, it's a must-do experience for anyone wanting to see The City Beautiful from new heights.

Hours	Times vary, typically 2 p.m. – 8 p.m.
Phone	321-209-9679
Location	8449 International Drive, Orlando, FL 32819
Website	theorlandoeye.com

Suggested Supplies

Small backpack or sling bag (valuables/supplies)	Binoculars	Bug repellant
Comfortable walking shoes	Stroller or wagon for kids	Snacks
Water—only 2 liters per person allowed.		

Winter Park, Florida

Total day trip time: approximately 2 hours. 40-minute round-trip drive, leaving 1 /14+ for the boat tour.

Dogs: No

- **Fees:**
  - o $20.00 Adults
  - o $10.00 Children (ages 2 through 11)
  - o $0 Children under 2
- **Activities**: Boat tour, wildlife viewing, architecture viewing

A Tranquil Cruise Through Old Florida Charm

Tucked away just north of Orlando, Winter Park's Scenic Boat Tour offers a peaceful, picture-perfect escape from the hustle and bustle of the theme parks. This relaxing, hour-long cruise takes visitors through a series of interconnected lakes and historic canals, revealing the natural beauty, elegant estates, and rich history that make Winter Park one of Florida's most charming hidden gems.

As the pontoon boat drifts away from the dock, guests are immediately immersed in a world of lush landscapes, sparkling water, and towering cypress trees draped in Spanish moss. The tour winds through the pristine waters of the Winter Park Chain of Lakes, with the captain narrating fascinating stories about the area's past, its famous residents, and the stunning homes that line the shore.

One of the highlights of the tour is gliding through the narrow, man-made canals originally built in the 1800s to connect the lakes. Overhanging trees create a natural tunnel, and the gentle ripples of the water provide a calm, meditative experience as the boat moves from one lake to the next. Along the way, wildlife is abundant, with graceful herons, sunbathing turtles, and even the occasional alligator making an appearance.

A View of Historic Mansions and Local Landmarks

Winter Park has long been known as a retreat for the wealthy. Many of these homes date back to the early 20th century, showcasing Mediterranean Revival architecture, sprawling lawns, and private boathouses.

Beyond the grand estates, visitors will also see Rollins College, one of Florida's oldest and most picturesque college campuses, as well as landmarks like Kraft Azalea Gardens, where towering cypress trees frame the shoreline.

A Relaxing Alternative to Orlando's Fast-Paced Attractions

For those seeking a slower, more intimate experience of Florida, the Scenic Boat Tour of Winter Park is the perfect getaway. With its gentle pace, breathtaking scenery, and rich storytelling, it's an ideal way to unwind, take in the sights, and discover a side of Central Florida that many visitors miss. Whether you're a nature lover, history buff, or just looking for a peaceful break from the crowds, this charming boat tour offers a slice of Old Florida charm that lingers long after the cruise is over.

Hours	10 a.m. – 4 p.m.
Phone	407-644-4056
Location	312 East Morse Blvd. Winter Park, FL 32789
Website	scenicboattours.com

Suggested Supplies

Sunscreen	Water	Bug repellant
Binoculars	Sunglasses	Snacks

Orlando, Florida

Total day trip time: approximately 6-10 hours. 40-minute round-trip drive, leaving 5+ hours for luxurious, pampered fun. You'll want to use all the time allowed at this park.

Dogs: No

- **Fees:**
  - $240.00+ (This is an **all-inclusive** park. Prices depend on package, dates and specials. Military discounts are available. See the website for pricing and booking.)
- **Activities:** Full day of swimming, wildlife encounters—swim with dolphins, food and drink.

All-Inclusive Relaxation Among Wildlife and Water Fun

For those seeking an unforgettable, all-inclusive experience in Orlando, Discovery Cove offers a tropical oasis unlike any other. Tucked away from the crowds and long lines of the city's theme parks, this exclusive day resort allows guests to swim with dolphins, snorkel among vibrant marine life, and relax on white sandy beaches—all while enjoying first-class service and unlimited food and drinks.

One of the most magical moments at Discovery Cove is the opportunity to swim with a dolphin. This signature experience brings guests face-to-face with these intelligent and playful creatures, where they can interact, learn about their behaviors, and even experience a gentle dorsal fin tow across the lagoon.

Beyond the dolphin encounter, Discovery Cove is a snorkeler's dream. The Grand Reef is teeming with colorful tropical fish and graceful rays, offering a chance to glide through crystal-clear waters and explore an underwater world. The experience is designed for all skill levels, making it perfect for both first-time snorkelers and experienced swimmers.

For those looking for a more tranquil adventure, the Freshwater Oasis provides a lazy-river-style journey through winding waterways, passing hidden grottos and lush rainforests where guests can spot playful otters and curious marmosets. The Serenity Bay and its pristine white beaches offer a relaxing escape, with hammocks swaying in the breeze and cabanas available for a truly VIP experience.

An Immersive Experience with Marine Life

Unlike most theme parks, Discovery Cove is designed to be a stress-free, all-inclusive retreat. Admission includes freshly prepared meals, snacks, and drinks throughout the day, allowing visitors to savor gourmet dishes, tropical drinks, and even frozen cocktails without worrying about extra costs. From breakfast by the water to mid-afternoon refreshments, every detail is taken care of.

The limited daily capacity ensures that the park never feels crowded, making it one of Orlando's most peaceful and exclusive attractions. Whether you're floating in a lagoon, snorkeling with exotic fish, or simply lounging under the palm trees, Discovery Cove offers a luxurious and immersive experience that feels worlds away from the usual theme park hustle.

Whether you're celebrating a special occasion, seeking an unforgettable family adventure, or simply looking to escape the ordinary, Discovery Cove is an experience unlike any other in Florida. With its exotic marine encounters, all-inclusive amenities, and lush tropical surroundings, it's the perfect place to relax, explore, and create lifelong memories in a paradise all your own.

Hours	8:00 a.m. - 5:00 p.m. daily. Check-in begins at 7:15 a.m.
Phone	407-513-4600
Location	6000 Discovery Cove Way, Orlando, FL 32821
Website	discoverycove.com

Suggested Supplies

Sunglasses	Change of clothes or wrap for dining	Swimsuit
Water shoes	Slip-on dry shoes	Sun hat

Note: This is an all-inclusive park which provides the use of lockers, wetsuit, towels, mask, shower amenities, souvenir snorkel, food, snacks, non-alcoholic beverages and select beers and wines.

Kissimmee, Florida

Total day trip time: approximately 4 hours. 1-hour drive round trip, leaving 3 hours for heart-pounding fun.

Dogs: Yes (**Warning,** there are unleashed dogs on the site) if accompanied on a leash.

- **Fees**
  - $59.95 Adult
  - $46.95 Ages 9-11

Military/senior discounts available.

Reservations are required. Must weigh **275 lbs or less** to participate.

  - **Locker** $3:00
  - **Climbing gloves** $2:00
- **Activities:** Physical challenge courses, ziplines.

A Thrilling Aerial Escape in the Treetops

For those looking to trade theme park lines for treetop thrills, Orlando Tree Trek Adventure Park offers a high-flying experience unlike any other. Just outside the city, this outdoor adventure course lets visitors climb, swing, and zip through a dense pine forest, providing an adrenaline-packed way to explore Florida's natural beauty from above.

Set on 15 acres of towering trees, the park features a series of progressively challenging obstacle courses, designed to test balance, strength, and bravery. Each self-guided course takes adventurers through a maze of swinging logs, suspended bridges, cargo nets, climbing walls, and ziplines, all set high above the forest floor. With courses designed for all skill levels, it's the perfect spot for families, thrill-seekers, and anyone ready to push their limits in a safe, controlled environment.

The Courses: Choose Your Challenge

Orlando Tree Trek Adventure Park features four adult courses and three kids' courses, ensuring that every visitor—whether a beginner or an experienced climber—finds the right challenge.

Beginner (Green) Course – A great introduction to treetop adventure, with easy crossings and lower heights to help build confidence.

Intermediate (Blue) Course – A step up in difficulty, featuring higher obstacles and more demanding elements.

Advanced (Silver) Course – Suspended even higher in the trees, this course challenges visitors with longer crossings and trickier balance obstacles.

Expert (Red) Course – The ultimate challenge, with extreme climbs, unpredictable elements, and a thrilling 425-foot zipline finale.

Junior and Kids' Courses – Designed specifically for younger adventurers (must be 6-8 years of age), these lower-to-the-ground courses offer a taste of aerial adventure while ensuring maximum safety.

Beyond the exhilarating obstacles, the real magic of Orlando Tree Trek is the immersive experience in nature. The fresh air, towering trees, and quiet sounds of the forest create a welcome escape from the bustle of Orlando's theme parks. Whether you're zipping between trees, tackling a wobbly suspension bridge, or conquering a cargo net, the sense of achievement and exhilaration makes it an unforgettable day trip.

If you don't want to participate, but just watch family or friends, there are walking trails along the course that allow you to walk and observe others as they use and progress through the courses.

With high-quality safety harnesses, expert guides, and a gradual progression of challenges, anyone can feel comfortable taking to the treetops. Whether you're visiting solo, with family, or in a group, Orlando Tree Trek Adventure Park offers a unique, exciting, and active way to experience Florida's great outdoors.

Hours	Daily from 8 a.m. Groups depart every 30 minutes. Last departure time and days open varies by season, so always go on-line to verify availability.
Phone	407-390-9999
Location	7625 Sinclair Rd. Kissimmee, Florida 34747
Website	orlandotreetrek.com

Suggested Supplies

Sunscreen	Water	Bug repellant
Snacks	Climbing gloves (available on-site $2)	

Note: Appropriate footwear and appropriate clothing (no loose clothing, dangling jewelry) are required for safety purposes. It is recommended that you wear clothing that you don't mind getting dirty (you're outside, it just happens). Guests may be refused access to the course if they do not have appropriate clothing that meets our safety standards.

Titusville, Florida

Total day trip time: approximately 5-7 hours. 2-hour drive round trip, leaving 5 hours for wildlife viewing and bioluminescence tour.
Dogs: Yes

- **Fees**
  - $10.00 per car. Military/Veterans can receive a free annual pass.
  - **Bioluminescence kayak tours:** From $60.00 up
- **Activities:** Hiking, biking, boating, wildlife viewing, birdwatching, auto touring.

Where Wilderness Meets the Space Coast

Just minutes from the launch pads of Kennedy Space Center, Merritt Island National Wildlife Refuge feels like a world apart—a sprawling sanctuary of marshes, coastal dunes, pine flatwoods, and hardwood hammocks where wildlife thrives and time slows down. Covering over 140,000 acres, this refuge is one of Florida's most diverse and ecologically important landscapes, offering a chance to experience Florida as it once was, long before rockets lit up the sky.

Originally created as a buffer zone for NASA in the 1960s, the refuge has since become a haven for more than 1,500 species of plants and animals, including manatees, alligators, bobcats, and over 350 species of birds—making it one of the best birdwatching spots in the southeastern U.S.

A great place to start your visit is the Visitor Information Center, which has exhibits, maps, and helpful rangers ready to point you in the right direction. From there, you can choose your adventure:

Black Point Wildlife Drive is a must-do: a 7-mile one-way road through marshes and shallow wetlands where you can see alligators sunning, roseate spoonbills feeding, and perhaps even a bald eagle perched in the distance. It's a relaxing, drive-at-your-own-pace experience, with pull-offs and observation platforms along the way.

For hikers, the refuge offers miles of nature trails, including the Oak and Palm Hammock Trails, which take you through shaded forests teeming with wildlife. You might spot armadillos rustling in the underbrush or hear ospreys calling overhead.

If you're on the water, the Mosquito Lagoon and Indian River Lagoon are perfect for kayaking or canoeing. These calm, shallow waters are home to dolphins, manatees, and even the magical bioluminescence that lights up the lagoon on warm summer nights.

Photographers and wildlife lovers will find inspiration around every bend, especially during sunrise and sunset, when the skies turn brilliant colors and the water reflects the beauty of the marsh.

There's something wonderfully wild and peaceful about Merritt Island. It's one of those rare places where you might see a rocket launch and a flock of roseate spoonbills in the same day. Whether you're exploring by car, foot, or kayak, this living landscape is a reminder of Florida's raw, untamed beauty—and how close it still is, just off the beaten path.

Bioluminescent Bay in Titusville: Florida's Magical Nighttime Light Show

As the sun sets over Merritt Island National Wildlife Refuge, the landscape begins to shift. The birds quiet down, the air cools, and the water takes on a mysterious, glassy stillness. But something extraordinary is about to happen—because after dark, these waters come alive in a way few expect.

Dip your paddle into the Indian River Lagoon or Mosquito Lagoon and watch as soft blue-green light swirls around it, glowing with every stroke. This is Florida's bioluminescence, one of nature's most enchanting light shows, and you're already in the perfect place to experience it.

The glow comes from dinoflagellates, microscopic plankton that emit light when disturbed. Each movement—whether from your kayak paddle, a jumping fish, or even your hand trailing through the water—leaves a glowing trail behind. On the darkest summer nights, it's so bright it looks like stardust dancing across the lagoon. In the cooler months, bioluminescent comb jellies take center stage, their glow more subtle and dreamy, like little lanterns drifting just beneath the surface.

Guided bioluminescent kayak and paddleboard tours often launch right from the refuge or nearby Haulover Canal, taking you deep into the calm backwaters under a starry sky. The best viewing is during a new moon, when the lack of light pollution allows the bioluminescence to shine in full effect. Tours usually last 90 minutes to two hours and are beginner-friendly, led by naturalist guides who share stories about the science and magic behind the glow.

It's hard to capture this experience in photos—but you'll never forget it. As you glide quietly across the lagoon, with nothing but the sound of frogs, crickets, and your own breath, each glowing swirl feels like a secret from the natural world. For many, it's a peaceful, almost spiritual encounter with Florida's wilder side.

Whether you're a seasoned paddler or trying it for the first time, witnessing the bioluminescence at Merritt Island is one of those rare Florida experiences that feels like discovering something truly hidden—and truly magical.

Hours	Refuge: Sunrise to sunset daily Visitor center: Tuesday through Saturday 8 a.m. until 4 p.m.
Phone	321-861-0667
Location	1963 Refuge Headquarters Road Titusville,FL32782
Website	.fws.gov/refuge/merritt-island

Bioluminescence Kayak Tours

BK Adventures (clear kayaks)	bkadventure.com
Florida Bioluminescence Tours	bioluminescencetours.com/

Suggested Supplies

Hiking boots/Comfortable shoes	Bug repellant	Sunscreen
Water	Snacks	Picnic supplies
Binoculars	Water shoes or old sneakers (kayaking)	Waterproof bags (kayaking) (gallon Ziplocks work well)

Kissimmee, Florida

Total day trip time: approximately 6 hours. 1-hour drive round trip, leaving 5 hours for alligator viewing and heart-thumping adventure.

Dogs: No

- **Fees:**
  - **Daily Admission**
    - $34.99 Adult (ages 13 and up)
    - $24.99 Child (ages 3-12)
    - $31.98 Senior (ages 60+)
  - **Off-Road Adventure Ride (includes daily admission)**
    - $46.99 Adult (13+)
    - $36.99 Child (3-12)
  - **Croc Rock Adventure (rock climb, bridge, zipline)**
    - Starting at $44.00 (includes daily admission)
  - **Activities:** Alligator shows, zipline, Off-road ride, rock climbing.

A Classic Florida Adventure with a Wild Side

For those looking for a taste of Old Florida charm mixed with thrilling wildlife encounters, Gatorland in Kissimmee delivers a one-of-a-kind experience. Founded in 1949, this iconic roadside attraction-turned-wildlife park has been welcoming visitors for over 75 years, earning its reputation as the "Alligator Capital of the World." While many of Florida's classic attractions have faded into history, Gatorland has stood the test of time, growing into a beloved destination for families, animal lovers, and adventure seekers alike.

Spread across 110 acres, Gatorland is home to thousands of alligators and crocodiles, from tiny hatchlings to massive 14-foot giants. The wooden boardwalks that wind through the park let visitors safely observe these prehistoric reptiles in their natural habitats, lounging in the sun, gliding through the water, or lurking just beneath the surface. Some of the most famous residents are the park's rare white alligators, a sight you won't see anywhere else.

Beyond the gators, the park offers a surprising variety of other wildlife, including Florida panthers, bobcats, tortoises, snakes, and exotic birds. The free-flight aviary lets guests walk among colorful, chirping tropical birds, while the petting zoo gives kids a chance to meet friendly farm animals up close.

Live Shows and Thrills

Gatorland isn't just about looking at alligators—it's about getting up close to them. Daily live shows like the Gator Jumparoo showcase these powerful predators launching themselves out of the water for food, while the Alligator Wrestling Show offers a closer-than-comfortable look at the skills once used by Florida's original gator trappers. For the bravest visitors, the Trainer-for-a-Day program provides a hands-on experience, allowing guests to interact with and even feed these incredible creatures under expert supervision.

If you're craving even more excitement, Gatorland has a thrill-seeker's side. The Screamin' Gator Zip Line sends guests soaring over pools filled with alligators, offering a bird's-eye view of the park with an added adrenaline rush. The Croc Rock Climbing Wall and Adventure Course provide yet another way to test your nerve in a setting unlike any other.

Despite being one of Central Florida's most famous attractions, Gatorland isn't as packed as the major theme parks, making it a refreshing alternative to long lines and crowds. While it's popular on weekends and during school breaks, it still offers a more relaxed, old-school Florida experience—one where you can take your time, enjoy the exhibits, and really soak in the atmosphere.

For visitors who want an authentic Florida experience, Gatorland is a must-visit destination. It blends history, nature, and adventure, offering close encounters with wildlife and plenty of excitement without the theme park chaos. Whether you're a first-time visitor or someone returning to relive childhood memories, Gatorland continues to be a wild and unforgettable adventure—just as it has been since 1949.

Hours	Daily 10 a.m.-5 p.m.
Phone	407-855-5496
Location	7625 Sinclair Rd. Kissimmee, Florida 34747
Website	gatorland.com

Suggested Supplies

Comfortable shoes	No outside food or drink allowed. Concessions on-site.	Sunscreen
Bug repellant	Sunglasses	Binoculars

De Leon Springs, Florida

Total day trip time: approximately 5 hours. 1 ½-hour drive round trip, leaving 3 ½ hours for swimming, paddling, and history.
Dogs: Yes (not allowed in water or buildings)
- **Fees:**
  - $6.00 per vehicle (two to eight people).
  - $4.00 single-occupant vehicle.
  - $4.00 motorcycle.
  - $2.00 pedestrian, bicyclist, and extra passengers.
- **Activities:** Swimming, paddling, hiking, and history

Swim in a Blend of Natural Beauty and Rich History

With so many stunning natural springs around Orlando, it's no surprise that they tend to draw big crowds. But De Leon Springs State Park stands out not just for its cool, crystal-clear waters, but also for its deep historical roots. This hidden gem offers a chance to swim, paddle, and explore while also uncovering the fascinating stories of the land's past—from Native American settlements to Spanish explorers and even a 19th-century resort.

The spring itself is a refreshing 72 degrees year-round, providing the perfect escape from Florida's heat. While it may not be as large as some of the region's better-known springs, its serene setting and fewer crowds make it a fantastic alternative for those looking to relax, swim, and soak in the natural surroundings. The waters flow into Spring Garden Run, a waterway that leads to Lake Woodruff National Wildlife Refuge, offering excellent paddling opportunities along cypress-lined trails teeming with wildlife.

What makes De Leon Springs truly unique is its rich history. This land has been inhabited for thousands of years, first by the Mayaca people, who thrived around the springs. Later, Spanish explorers arrived, believing they had found the legendary Fountain of Youth. In the 1800s, the area was transformed into a plantation, a tourist resort, and even a health spa, drawing visitors seeking relaxation and rejuvenation.

Today, remnants of this past can still be seen throughout the park, including interpretive displays and walking trails that highlight the area's Native American, Spanish, and early American history.

Beyond swimming and history, De Leon Springs offers kayaking, canoeing, and hiking trails that wind through lush hammocks and cypress swamps. And for those who love a unique dining experience, the famous Old Spanish Sugar Mill restaurant, located inside the park, lets visitors grill their own pancakes at their table, making for a one-of-a-kind meal in a beautiful setting.

For those looking for a spring experience with a little more character, De Leon Springs provides the best of both worlds—a place to cool off in pristine waters while also diving into Florida's rich and complex history. Whether you're swimming, paddling, or simply wandering the historic grounds, it's a destination that offers a glimpse into the past alongside the beauty of the present.

Hours	8 a.m. to Sunset daily
Phone	386-985-4212
Location	601 Ponce De Leon Blvd De Leon Springs, Fl 32130
Website	floridastateparks.org/parks-and-trails/de-leon-springs-state-park

Suggested Supplies

Water	Snacks	Picnic supplies
Blanket/chairs	Masks/snorkels/fins	Floats
Sunscreen	Towels	Change of clothes
Binoculars	Waste pick-up bags for Fido	Wipes (because nature can be dirty!)

Kissimmee, Florida

Total day trip time: approximately 5 hours. 1 ½-hours' drive round trip, leaving 3 1/2 for fun and exploring.
Dogs: Yes
- **Fees:**
  - $0
- **Activities:** Walking, biking, paddling, picnicking

The Gateway to the Everglades

Hidden just minutes from the hustle of Orlando's theme parks, Shingle Creek offers a peaceful escape into Florida's wild and natural beauty. Known as the northernmost headwaters of the Everglades, this scenic waterway winds through lush cypress forests, freshwater marshes, and winding trails, making it a perfect destination for paddling, hiking, fishing, and wildlife viewing.

One of the best ways to explore Shingle Creek is by kayak, canoe, or paddleboard, gliding through narrow waterways shaded by towering cypress trees draped in Spanish moss. The creek's calm waters make it beginner-friendly, yet still offer plenty of adventure for experienced paddlers. As you navigate the twists and turns, keep an eye out for turtles, otters, herons, egrets, and even alligators sunning themselves along the banks.

Several launch points and rental facilities make it easy to get on the water, with routes ranging from short paddles to half-day excursions deep into Florida's wetlands.

Kissimmee River Kayak LLC at the Paddling Center offer canoe, single and double kayak and stand-up paddle board rentals as well as guided tours and lessons. Prices start at $20 for the first hour for paddle boards and $30 for the first two hours for kayaks.

For those who prefer to stay on land, Shingle Creek features well-maintained trails that wind through pine forests, cypress swamps, and open marshlands. Whether you're looking for a leisurely nature walk or a longer bike ride, the trails offer plenty of opportunities to spot wildlife, take in scenic views, and enjoy the fresh air.

The Shingle Creek Regional Trail, a multi-use pathway, connects several parks and natural areas, making it an ideal route for biking, jogging, or birdwatching.

Despite its proximity to Orlando's major attractions, Shingle Creek remains peaceful and uncrowded, making it a perfect retreat for those looking to escape the theme park crowds. Whether you're floating down the creek, trekking through shaded trails, or simply soaking in the natural beauty, Shingle Creek offers a glimpse into Florida's wild side—just a stone's throw from the city.

Hours	Dawn to dusk daily
Phone	407-742-0335
Location	2491 Babb Road, Kissimmee, Fl 34746
Website	osceola.org/Community/Parks-and-Conservation-Lands/Find-a-Park-Facility-or-Conservation-Area/Shingle-Creek-Regional-Park

Suggested Supplies

Sunscreen	Bug repellant	Snacks
Picnic supplies (grills available)	Waste pick-up bags for Fido	Binoculars
Backpack	Wipes	Water shoes or old sneakers (paddling)
Waterproof bags (Ziplocks work well)	Sunglasses	Chairs/blanket (picnicking)

Apopka, Florida

Total day trip time: approximately 5 hours. 2-hour round-trip drive, leaving 3 hours for peaceful fun.
Dogs: Yes (Please take caution near the water's edge!)
- **Fees:**
  - $0
- **Activities**: Wildlife viewing, hiking, biking, driving tour.

A Scenic Escape for Hikers and Wildlife Enthusiasts

For those seeking a quiet, immersive nature experience, Lake Apopka North Shore offers some of the best hiking and wildlife viewing in Central Florida. Once a thriving agricultural area, this restored landscape has been transformed into a vast wetlands sanctuary, rich in biodiversity and teeming with wildlife. Whether hiking along the trails or driving the renowned Wildlife Drive, visitors can explore miles of open marshes, cypress-lined shores, and panoramic lake views, all while spotting an incredible variety of birds and animals.

Hiking Through a Birdwatcher's Paradise

The hiking trails at Lake Apopka North Shore wind through an ever-changing landscape of marshes, canals, and wetlands, offering a peaceful retreat into nature. As you walk along the raised levees, water stretches endlessly on both sides, creating a perfect habitat for wading birds, alligators, and turtles basking in the sun.

Birdwatchers, in particular, will find this area exceptional, as the region is home to over 360 bird species, making it one of Florida's premier birding destinations. Visitors may spot roseate spoonbills, great blue herons, anhingas, and even rare sightings like the snail kite or bald eagle. During the winter months, migratory flocks fill the skies, adding to the already impressive wildlife spectacle.

The flat, well-maintained trails make for an easy and enjoyable hike, whether you're out for a short stroll or a longer trek. Along the way, the scenery shifts from open water vistas to shady tree tunnels, with plenty of opportunities to stop, take photos, and simply soak in the serenity of this untouched landscape.

The Wildlife Drive: A Safari-Like Adventure

For those who prefer to explore from the comfort of their car, the Lake Apopka Wildlife Drive offers a spectacular 11-mile journey through the wetlands, providing up-close encounters with Florida's natural beauty. The slow-moving, one-way drive allows visitors to take their time, roll down the windows, and observe wildlife at their own pace.

Alligators are frequently seen sunbathing along the canals, sometimes lined up in astonishing numbers along the banks. Birds swoop overhead, and turtles peek out from the water's edge. The peacefulness of the drive makes it a favorite for photographers and nature enthusiasts, who can capture breathtaking shots without leaving their vehicle. There are several designated pull-off areas along the route, allowing visitors to step out, take in the scenery, and enjoy the quiet sounds of nature.

Whether exploring on foot or by car, Lake Apopka North Shore offers a rare glimpse into Florida's untamed wilderness, free from crowds and distractions. Here, the sound of rustling reeds replaces the noise of the city, and the sight of a soaring osprey or a sunbathing gator reminds visitors of nature's quiet wonders. With expansive views, abundant wildlife, and a sense of solitude, it's a place where you can truly slow down, breathe deeply, and reconnect with the natural world.

Hours	Sunrise to sunset daily
Phone	407-254-9046
Location	2850 Lust Road, Apopka, FL 32703
Website	sjrwmd.com/lands/recreation/lake-apopka/

Suggested Supplies

Water	Snacks	Binoculars
Hiking boots/comfortable shoes	Sunscreen	Waste disposal bags for Fido
Bug repellant	Sunglasses	Wipes

Loving the Adventure So Far?

If you've discovered a new favorite spot, found the perfect quiet trail, or just love flipping through the pages of *Florida Day Trip Adventures*, I'd be so grateful if you'd leave a quick review.

It doesn't have to be long—just a sentence or two is enough to help others find this book and start their own journeys. Reviews make a huge difference in helping readers (and fellow explorers!) discover the hidden Florida we love.

Use your phone's camera to scan the QR code below to leave your review.

Thanks so much for being part of this adventure!
—Janice

Tampa

Tampa isn't your typical Florida city. Yes, it has sunshine, palm trees, and waterfront views—but it also has depth. Spanish-Cuban history blends with modern energy, and wild nature sits surprisingly close to downtown. One moment you're deciding between paddleboarding at sunrise or exploring a quiet preserve; the next, you're grabbing a Cuban sandwich in Ybor City.

For outdoor lovers, Tampa offers far more than good weather. Paddle through mangrove tunnels at Weedon Island Preserve or climb the observation tower for sweeping bay views. Wander the shaded trails at Eureka Springs Park or stroll the boardwalk at Lettuce Lake Conservation Park, where alligators, turtles, and wading birds are regular sightings. Kayaks are available onsite, making it easy to slip into a peaceful stretch of the Hillsborough River.

Just outside the city, Hillsborough River State Park delivers a taste of Old Florida, with forested trails, historic fort remains, and even rare Class II rapids. Fort De Soto Park offers beaches, paddling, and one of Florida's best dog-friendly stretches of sand. Families can connect with animals at HorsePower for Kids & Animal Sanctuary or enjoy up-close encounters at ZooTampa and the Florida Aquarium.

For something unexpected, City Escape Adventures turns downtown into an interactive puzzle, while TreeHoppers challenges visitors to climb and zip through the treetops.

Whether you're hiking in solitude, kayaking through bird-filled wetlands, or relaxing by the bay, Tampa offers both energy and escape—often in the same afternoon. It's a city of contrasts, surprises, and quiet corners, if you know where to look.

Tampa, Florida

Total day trip time: approximately 1 ½ to 2 ¼ hours. 6-minute drive round trip, leaving 1-2 hours for adventure (games range from 1-2 hours in length.

Dogs: Yes (not recommended)

- **Fees:**
  - $39.00
- **Activity:** Escape room adventure outdoors.

Tampa's Outdoor Puzzle Quest

If you're looking for a fun and unconventional way to explore Tampa, City Escape Adventures delivers a dynamic twist on sightseeing with a two-hour outdoor escape experience that unfolds along the city's scenic Riverwalk. Designed for those who love riddles, teamwork, and discovering hidden gems, this immersive scavenger-style adventure transforms Tampa into a real-life puzzle board.

Instead of being locked in a room like a traditional escape game, you and your team will roam the downtown streets, solving clues, unraveling storylines, and interacting with augmented reality elements that add a layer of excitement to your mission. Along the way, you'll be challenged to notice the details hiding in plain sight—from historic landmarks to surprising symbols—while piecing together a story that's part mystery, part city tour.

Each game is crafted with a unique storyline, and the puzzles are designed to be clever and collaborative—perfect for friends, families, tourists, or even coworkers looking for a creative team-building experience. As you make your way along the Riverwalk, you'll not only get caught up in the game but also catch glimpses of Tampa's waterfront beauty, street art, and architectural charm.

It's more than just a walk in the city—it's an engaging mental and physical adventure where the streets of Tampa become your playing field. Whether you're a local ready to rediscover familiar streets or a visitor wanting to see the city from a whole new angle, City Escape Adventures is a memorable and energizing way to spend an afternoon outdoors, solving puzzles and making memories.

Hours	Monday-Saturday 10 a.m.-4 p.m. Sunday 12 p.m.-4 p.m.
Phone	813-789-8101
Location	400 North Ashley Street, Suite #1900 Tampa, FL 33602
Website	can-you-escape.com/

Suggested Supplies

Water	Bug repellant	Comfortable shoes and clothing
Sunscreen	Waste pick-up bags if Fido joins you	Paper and pencil/pen (for clues and notes)

Tampa, Florida

Total day trip time: approximately 2 1/2 hours. 15-minute round-trip drive, 1 ½-hour tour, allowing time to arrive early.
Dogs: Yes
- **Fees:**
  - $25.00 Adults
  - $12.00 Children
- **Activities:** Sightseeing boat ride, dolphin watching

The Ultimate Scenic Cruise Experience

Set sail on the Tampa Bay Fun Boat, where sightseeing, relaxation, and waterfront adventure come together for an unforgettable experience. Departing from the marina behind the Tampa Convention Center, this 36-foot deck boat offers a unique way to explore downtown Tampa's scenic waterways. Whether you're looking for a leisurely cruise or a vibrant sunset experience, Tampa Bay Fun Boat delivers a perfect blend of sightseeing, fun, and laid-back Florida vibes.

As the boat glides along the bay, passengers are treated to stunning views of Tampa's skyline, historic sites, and local wildlife. The 90-minute sightseeing cruise is a relaxing way to take in the area's iconic landmarks, while the captain shares interesting stories and historical facts about the city. Dolphins, manatees, and seabirds frequently make appearances, adding to the magic of the journey. The atmosphere is enhanced with curated music selections, and guests can enjoy complimentary bottled water while soaking in the sun and the sights.

Sunset Cruises: A Picture-Perfect Ending

For those looking for a more romantic or peaceful experience, the Sunset Cruise offers a breathtaking view of the sky as it transforms into hues of orange, pink, and purple over Tampa Bay. The gentle movement of the boat combined with the golden glow of the setting sun makes for a spectacular way to wind down the day.

Tampa Bay Fun Boat isn't just a tour—it's an experience. Whether you're cruising past Tampa's skyline, watching for dolphins, or simply unwinding on the water, this boat offers a relaxed and fun way to explore the city from a whole new perspective. It's a must-do for visitors and locals alike, offering a refreshing escape from the crowds and a front-row seat to Tampa's stunning waterfront beauty.

Hours	Hours vary—check website
Phone	727-204-9787
Location	333 S Franklin St, Tampa, FL 33602
Website	tampabayfunboat.com

Suggested Supplies

Snacks (no food available on board)	Sunscreen	Bug repellant
Binoculars	Waste pick-up bags for Fido	Sunglasses

Tampa, Florida

Total day trip time: approximately 2 hours. 30-minute drive round trip, leaving 1 ½ hours for a leisurely stroll.
Dogs: Yes
- **Fees:**
  o $2.00 per vehicle. Up to 8 people per vehicle.
- **Activities:** walking, plant and wildlife viewing

Easy, Peaceful Walk in a Hidden Botanical Gem in Tampa

Tucked away just east of downtown Tampa, Eureka Springs Park is a peaceful and unexpected escape, known for its lush greenery, quiet walking trails, and the only publicly owned botanical garden in Hillsborough County. Originally founded in the 1930s by amateur botanist Albert Greenberg, this serene 31-acre park began as a private tropical plant nursery and orchid garden, and it still retains that tranquil, cultivated charm today.

Visitors are welcomed by a charming greenhouse and winding boardwalks that lead through a cypress and tupelo swamp, where the rustling of leaves and the calls of birds fill the air. The botanical garden, though modest in size, showcases an array of tropical plants, colorful blooms, and mature ferns that give the park a quiet, almost enchanted feel. Benches and shaded nooks invite guests to pause, reflect, or enjoy a good book surrounded by nature.

The park also features a short system of walking trails, a small butterfly garden, and several picturesque wooden bridges that cross calm, reflective ponds. Photographers and nature lovers often visit for the chance to see native birds and other wildlife in a more manicured, but still natural, setting.

Eureka Springs Park is not a high-traffic destination, which is part of its charm. It's an ideal spot for those seeking a leisurely stroll, a quiet picnic, or a moment of solitude among flowers and ferns. With its gentle trails, tropical plantings, and sense of old Florida charm, this little park feels like a well-kept secret—one you'll be glad you discovered.

Hours	8 a.m. to 6 p.m. daily
Phone	813-744-5536
Location	6400 Eureka Springs Rd. Tampa, FL 33610
Website	hcfl.gov/locations/eureka-springs-conservation-park

Suggested Supplies

Water	Snacks	Bug repellant
Sunscreen	Binoculars	Stroller or wagon for kids
Waste pick-up bags for Fido	Walking shoes	

Tampa, Florida

Total day trip time: approximately 5 hours. 40-minute round-trip drive, leaving 4 ¼ hours for fun and exploring.

Dogs: Yes (not allowed on boardwalks or watercraft rentals)

- **Fees:**
  - $2.00 per vehicle Up to 8 people per vehicle
    - **Canoe/kayak rental** $25.00 for up to 4 hours. $10.00 per hour thereafter.
- **Activities**: Hiking, paddling, boardwalk, observation tower, playgrounds, wildlife viewing

A Natural Escape in Tampa

Tucked along the Hillsborough River, Lettuce Lake Conservation Park is a tranquil retreat just minutes from Tampa's city center. Covering 240 acres, this park offers a perfect blend of scenic beauty, outdoor recreation, and wildlife viewing, making it a favorite for hikers, paddlers, birdwatchers, and families looking to reconnect with nature.

A highlight of the park is its 3,500-foot boardwalk, which winds through a dense hardwood swamp, leading to a scenic observation tower overlooking the river. From this elevated vantage point, visitors can take in stunning panoramic views and often spot alligators, turtles, wading birds, and even the occasional manatee. The park also features a 1.25-mile paved exercise trail, ideal for walking, jogging, or biking, with fitness stations along the way for an extra challenge.

For those looking to explore the water, the park offers kayak and canoe rentals, making it easy to glide along the peaceful river and experience nature from a different perspective. The Hillsborough River is lined with towering cypress trees, lush greenery, and an abundance of wildlife, offering an immersive and relaxing paddling experience.

Families and groups will find plenty of shaded picnic areas throughout the park, complete with tables, barbecue grills, and pavilions—perfect for an afternoon gathering or a quiet lunch in nature. The park also features two playgrounds, one of which includes adaptive and sensory-friendly equipment, ensuring a fun and engaging space for children of all abilities.

With its scenic boardwalks, winding trails, and peaceful river views, Lettuce Lake Conservation Park is a hidden gem for anyone looking to escape into nature without leaving the city. Whether you're hiking under the shade of towering oaks, paddling along the winding river, or enjoying a quiet picnic, this park offers a refreshing break from the everyday and a chance to experience Florida's wild beauty up close.

Hours	Spring & Summer: 8:00 AM to 7:00 PMFall & Winter: 8:00 AM to 6:00 PM
Phone	813-987-6204
Location	6920 East Fletcher Avenue, Tampa, FL 33637
Website	hcfl.gov/locations/lettuce-lake-conservation-park

Suggested Supplies

Water	Sunscreen	Snacks
Binoculars	Stroller or wagon for children	Picnic supplies
Waste pick-up bags for Fido	Sunglasses	Bug repellant
Chairs/blanket (picnic)		

St. Petersburg, Florida

Total day trip time: approximately 3 hours. 1-hour round-trip drive, leaving 2 hours to explore the gardens and meet the wildlife.
Dogs: No (Only ADA dogs—no ESAs)
- **Fees:**
  - $15.00 Adults:
  - $12.00 Seniors (62+)
  - $6.00 Children (2-12)
- **Activities:** Horticulture and wildlife viewing

A Century-Old Florida Treasure

Long before Florida became synonymous with massive theme parks and modern attractions, Sunken Gardens was welcoming visitors into its lush tropical world. Established more than a century ago in St. Petersburg, this historic garden remains one of Florida's oldest living attractions—a peaceful retreat filled with exotic plants, winding paths, and gentle waterfalls.

The story began in the early 1900s when George Turner Sr., a local plumber with a passion for gardening, purchased four acres that included a shallow lake. After discovering rich soil beneath the surface, he drained the water and began planting tropical trees, flowering plants, and ferns. What started as a personal project gradually grew into a beloved destination, drawing curious visitors eager to experience its sunken, subtropical landscape.

Today, guests wander along brick pathways shaded by towering banyan trees and vibrant orchids. Butterflies drift through the air, while koi ponds, trickling streams, and small waterfalls create a calm, timeless atmosphere. One of the garden's most photographed features is its flock of flamingos—an enduring symbol of classic Florida charm.

Sunken Gardens is more than a botanical display; it's a living reminder of Florida's early tourism era. As one of the few remaining historic roadside attractions, it preserves the spirit of "Old Florida," when simple natural beauty was the main draw. The gardens continue to serve the community through horticultural workshops, educational programs, and special events, ensuring their legacy carries forward.

For more than 100 years, Sunken Gardens has offered visitors a quiet escape into tropical beauty. Whether you're drawn by the history, the plants, or the peaceful setting, it remains one of Florida's most memorable garden experiences.

Hours	Monday - Saturday: 10 a.m. - 4:30 p.m. Sunday: 12 p.m. - 4:30 p.m. The last admission is sold at 4 p.m. daily.
Phone	727-551-3102
Location	1825 4th St. N. St. Petersburg, FL 33704
Website	sunkengardens.org

Suggested Supplies

Water	Snacks	Sunscreen
Bug repellant	Comfortable walking shoes	Stroller or wagon for kids

St. Petersburg, Florida

Total day trip time: approximately 4-6 hours. 50-minute round-trip drive, leaving 4-5+ hours for exploring.

Dogs: No

- **Fees:**
  - $0
  - **Guided kayak** tours available starting at $45.00 (2.5 hours)
- **Activities:** Hiking, history, paddling, wildlife viewing, birdwatching.

Nature, History, and a Quiet Escape in St. Pete

Situated along the western shore of Tampa Bay in northeast St. Petersburg, Weedon Island Preserve is a serene retreat where natural beauty and ancient history blend seamlessly. With over 3,000 acres of coastal habitat, including mangrove forests, tidal creeks, pine flatwoods, and upland hammocks, this protected landscape is one of the most peaceful places to explore in the region.

Visitors come here to walk, paddle, birdwatch, and reflect. A network of well-maintained boardwalks and trails winds through the preserve, offering up-close views of native plants and wildlife, including roseate spoonbills, herons, and even the occasional dolphin or manatee cruising the shallows. Climb the observation tower, and you'll get a wide-open view of Tampa Bay stretching out in every direction. It's especially nice early in the morning or near sunset, when the light softens, and everything feels calmer. You may find yourself leaning on the railing longer than you expected, just taking it all in.

If you bring a kayak, the marked water trails are where this place really shines. The paddling routes are clearly labeled with numbered markers and signs, so you can relax and enjoy the ride instead of wondering which way to turn. As you glide into the narrow mangrove tunnels, everything gets quiet and shady. The water is usually calm, the air feels cooler under the canopy, and you'll hear birds rustling overhead or fish breaking the surface nearby. After a while, the outside world just fades away. It's peaceful in the best, simplest way.

Weedon Island isn't only about scenery. The Cultural and Natural History Center tells the story of the Weeden Island people who lived here more than a thousand years ago. Inside, you'll find pottery, tools, and exhibits that help you picture what life was like long before modern Tampa existed.

Whether you're walking the trails, paddling through the mangroves, or learning a bit of history along the way, Weedon Island gives you something we all need more of: room to slow down and enjoy where you are.

Hours	7 a.m. to 15 minutes before sundown daily
Phone	727-453-6500
Location	1800 Weedon Dr. NE, St. Petersburg, Florida, 33702
Website	weedonislandpreserve.org/

Kayak/canoe rental: https://ecomersion.com/

Suggested Supplies

Water	Snacks	Picnic supplies
Sunscreen	Bug repellant	Binoculars
Hiking boots/walking shoes	Water shoes (kayaking)	Waterproof bags for kayak trip (Ziplocks work fine)

Plant City, Florida

Total day trip time: approximately 4 hours. 1-hour drive round trip, leaving 3 hours for fun and exploring.

Dogs: Yes

- **Fees:**
  - $24.95 Adult
  - $19.95 Child (Ages 3-12 Children 2 and under are FREE)
  - $22.95 Senior
  - $5.00 **Train tickets**

Fees vary for other activities

- **Activities:** Nature walk among dinosaurs, hands-on exhibits, and activities

A Prehistoric Adventure Awaits

Step back in time and wander among towering dinosaurs at Dinosaur World Florida, an immersive outdoor park nestled in Plant City. This family-friendly destination is home to over 200 life-sized dinosaur replicas, set within a lush, natural landscape, offering a glimpse into a world that existed millions of years ago. Whether you're a dinosaur enthusiast, a curious explorer, or a family looking for a unique day trip, Dinosaur World provides a fun, hands-on experience that blends education with adventure.

As you stroll along the scenic pathways, you'll come face-to-face with impressively detailed dinosaur models, each accompanied by educational displays that share fascinating facts about their prehistoric reign. These giant creatures seem to come to life against a backdrop of towering trees and winding trails, making the park a true step into the past.

For those who love a little hands-on fun, Dinosaur World offers a variety of interactive exhibits:

Fossil Dig – Young paleontologists can dig through sand to unearth real fossils, including shark teeth, bone fragments, and ancient shells. Visitors can even take home three of their favorite discoveries as souvenirs. (Additional fee)

Dino Gem Excavation – Guests can sift through mining rough to uncover sparkling gems and minerals, mimicking the experience of treasure hunting. (Additional fee)

Prehistoric Museum – This indoor exhibit showcases a fascinating collection of fossils, animatronic dinosaurs, and full-scale skeletons, offering a deeper look at the creatures that once roamed the earth.

Dino-Themed Playgrounds – Children can run, climb, and explore specially designed play areas, complete with dinosaur structures and shaded seating areas for parents.

A Pet-Friendly Park

One of the unique features of Dinosaur World is its pet-friendly policy—leashed dogs are welcome to explore the outdoor exhibits alongside their human companions. Water stations are available throughout the park to keep pets comfortable, making this a rare attraction where the whole family, including furry friends, can enjoy the experience together.

Unlike traditional theme parks, Dinosaur World offers a more laid-back, natural experience, allowing visitors to wander at their own pace, take in the sights, and enjoy a picnic under the shade of the towering trees. While there are no food vendors on-site, guests are welcome to bring their own meals and snacks to enjoy at the designated picnic areas.

Perfect for families, school groups, and dinosaur enthusiasts of all ages, Dinosaur World Florida is a nostalgic nod to classic roadside attractions and a refreshing escape into prehistoric adventure. Whether you're digging for fossils, walking among life-sized dinosaurs, or marveling at ancient relics, it's an experience that brings the past to life in a way that's both fun and educational.

Hours	10 a.m. to 5 p.m. daily
Phone	813-717-9865
Location	5145 Harvey Tew Road Plant City, FL 33565
Website	dinosaurworld.com/florida

Suggested Supplies

Water	Snacks	Picnic supplies (**no food or drink available at the site**)
Sunscreen	Bug repellant	Stroller or wagon for kids
Waste pick-up bags for Fido	Wipes	Backpack or sling bag

Tampa, Florida

Total day trip time: approximately 4-5 hours. 1-hour round-trip drive, leaving 3 or 4 hours for play, petting, and learning.

Dogs: No

- **Fees:**
  - $14.00 Adults ($5.00 on 1st Thursday of each month)
  - $0 Children 12 months and under
    - **Pony rides:**
      - $5.00
- **Activities:** petting zoo, playground, **pony rides**

A Hands-On Farm Experience and Playground

If you're looking for a place where kids (and adults) can connect with animals, breathe in some fresh country air, and have a whole lot of fun, HorsePower for Kids & Animal Sanctuary in Tampa is the perfect day trip destination. More than just a petting zoo, this nonprofit organization offers a unique blend of animal rescue, education, and hands-on experiences in a warm, family-friendly environment.

As soon as you arrive, you'll be greeted by the sounds of clucking chickens, crowing roosters, and the gentle whinnies of horses in the distance. Spread out over open fields and shady groves, the sanctuary is home to rescued farm animals and exotic wildlife, including horses, goats, pigs, cows, donkeys, rabbits, llamas, emus, and even peacocks. Children can get up close and personal with many of these animals— petting, brushing, feeding, and learning their stories along the way.

One of the highlights for young visitors is the pony ride experience, where kids can saddle up and take a gentle ride around the farm. There's also a playground, shaded picnic areas, and a tractor-pulled hayride that takes guests on a loop around the sanctuary's scenic property.

But this place isn't just about fun—it's about compassion. HorsePower for Kids works to provide a safe haven for animals in need while also giving children, especially those who may not otherwise have access to rural life, a chance to connect with nature and animals in a meaningful way.

Whether you're visiting for a family day out, celebrating a birthday, or just in search of an old-fashioned good time, HorsePower for Kids offers a down-to-earth, heartfelt experience that's both entertaining and enriching. It's one of those places where kids get a little dirty, learn something new, and leave with big smiles—and maybe a little hay in their shoes.

Hours	Thursday/Friday 10 a.m. – 2 p.m. Saturday/Sunday 9 a.m. – 5 p.m.
Phone	813-855-8992
Location	8005 Racetrack Rd. Tampa, FL 33635
Website	horsepowerforkids.com/

Suggested Supplies

Snacks	Water	Bug repellant
Sunscreen	Close-toed shoes recommended	Picnic supplies (a great place for a picnic!)
Wipes	Picnic blanket	Sunglasses

Thonotosassa, Florida

Total day trip time: approximately 6 hours. 1 ½-hour drive round trip, leaving 4 ½ hours for fun and adventure.

Dogs: Yes

- **Fees:**
  - **Entrance:**
    - $6.00 per vehicle (up to eight people).
    - $4.00 single-occupant vehicle.
    - $2.00 pedestrians, bicyclists, extra passengers, passengers in a vehicle with a holder of an Annual Individual Entrance Pass.
  - **Bike Rental:**
    - Mountain bike: $15.00 per hour
    - Cruiser bike: $10.00 per hour
    - Child's bike: $10.00 per hour

Rental location: Park concessions in Parking Lot 4. Return rentals before the concession closes at 5 p.m.

  - **Canoe and Kayak Rentals:**
    - Up to four hours: $25.00
    - Hourly fee for each additional hour: $10.00

Rental location: Park concessionaire

- **Activities:** Hiking, biking, paddling, fishing, picnicking, wildlife viewing, history

Rapids, Trails, and Timeless Beauty—Just a Short Drive from Tampa.

Just a 45-minute drive from Tampa, Hillsborough River State Park offers a peaceful, adventure-filled day trip for anyone looking to reconnect with nature. One of Florida's original state parks, it's known for its surprising variety of landscapes—including something rare in this part of the state: rapids.

Here, the Hillsborough River flows swiftly over exposed limestone ledges, creating a series of bubbling rapids that wind through a forest of towering cypress and oak trees. The River Rapids Trail runs right alongside the water, offering a shady and scenic hike with plenty of spots to stop and take in the view.

If you're more at home on the water, rent a canoe or kayak and paddle down the calmer stretches of the river, where you might spot turtles, wading birds, or even an alligator or two basking in the sun. It's a peaceful, slow-moving route—perfect for beginners or families.

The park has nearly seven miles of hiking and biking trails, each one offering a different glimpse of Florida's natural beauty—from palm hammocks to hardwood forests. There are also boardwalks that wind through wetlands, making wildlife spotting easy and fun.

History lovers will enjoy visiting Fort Foster, a full-scale reconstruction of a military fort used during the Second Seminole War. On special weekends, costumed interpreters bring the site to life with live demonstrations and tours.

For families, the park includes a playground, picnic areas, and even a seasonal swimming pool, perfect for cooling off after a morning hike. With its mix of nature, history, and outdoor fun, Hillsborough River State Park makes a great day trip for anyone looking to slow down, explore, and experience a wilder side of Florida.

Hours	8 a.m. to sundown daily
Phone	813-688-9500
Location	15402 U.S. 301 North Thonotosassa FL 33592
Website	floridastateparks.org/parks-and-trails/hillsborough-river-state-park

Suggested Supplies

Sunscreen	Binoculars	Bug repellant
Helmets (if biking—required for children)	Hiking boots or good walking shoes	Water
Snacks	Picnic supplies	Water shoes or old sneakers if boating
Waste clean-up bags if Fido joins you	Picnic blanket/chairs	Waterproof bags if boating/fishing (Ziplocks work well)

Tierra Verde, Florida

Total day trip time: approximately 5 ½ hours. 1 ½-hour drive round trip, leaving 4 for fun and exploring.
Dogs: Yes—Dog Friendly Beach
- **Fees:**
  - $6.00 parking
- **Activities:** Hiking, water sports, swimming, dog beach

Leash Up for Trails and Let Loose at the Dog Beach—Fort De Soto Delivers Both

Sprawling across five interconnected keys at the southern tip of Pinellas County, Fort De Soto Park is a spectacular blend of pristine beaches, coastal wildlife, and rich history. With over 1,100 acres of protected land, this beloved destination offers something for every kind of outdoor enthusiast—whether you're looking to paddle through mangrove tunnels, wander through a historic fort, or simply sink your toes into sugar-white sand.

What makes Fort De Soto truly special is its sense of untouched Florida. The park's expansive coastline offers some of the most stunning beaches in the state, including its award-winning North Beach, often recognized for its clear, shallow waters, soft sand, and peaceful atmosphere. It's the perfect place for a family picnic, a swim, or a day spent beachcombing and dolphin-watching.

Paddlers and nature lovers can explore the canoe and kayak trails that wind through lush mangroves, while birdwatchers will find themselves in paradise—more than 300 species of birds have been recorded here, making it one of the top birding destinations in Florida. Hikers and cyclists can enjoy the park's 7-mile paved recreational trail, which connects the various keys and passes through shaded hammocks and along scenic waterfront views.

The park's namesake, Fort De Soto, dates back to the Spanish-American War and still stands with its original mortar battery, historic cannons, and sweeping views of Tampa Bay. Visitors can walk through its corridors and climb to the top of the ramparts for a glimpse into Florida's military past.

Another standout feature is the dog beach and Paw Playground, one of the few places in the region where dogs can play off-leash in the surf. With separate fenced areas for large and small dogs and freshwater showers to rinse them off afterward, it's a canine paradise.

Whether you're exploring the fort, kayaking through quiet coves, casting a fishing line from the long pier, or simply watching the sun dip below the Gulf horizon, Fort De Soto Park offers a day of adventure and tranquility wrapped in one of Florida's most scenic coastal settings. It's no wonder this place is a local favorite—and a must-visit for anyone seeking the quieter side of Florida's Gulf Coast.

Hours	7 a.m. to sunset daily
Phone	727-582-2100
Location	3500 Pinellas Bayway South, Tierra Verde, FL 33715
Website	pinellas.gov/parks/fort-de-soto-park

Suggested Supplies

Sunscreen	Water	Snacks (Concession stands on site)
Towels	Beach blanket	Chairs
Picnic supplies	Sunglasses	Sand/water shoes
Comfortable walking shoes for trails	Stroller or wagon for kids	Waste pick-up bags for Fido

Cortez, Florida

Total day trip time: approximately 6-8 hours. 2-hour round-trip drive, leaving 4-6 hours for exploring and adventure.
Dogs: Yes
- **Fees:**
  o Fees are dependent on the activities chosen
- **Activities:** Beaches, cycling, paddling, hiking, fresh seafood dining, fishing, tour boat rides, history.

Cortez, Florida: A Slice of Old Florida by the Sea

Tucked along the shimmering waters of Sarasota Bay, Cortez, Florida is one of the last remaining working fishing villages in the Sunshine State—a place where time seems to slow down, and the charm of "Old Florida" is alive and well. With its weathered wooden cottages, sun-bleached docks, and boats bobbing in the harbor, Cortez offers visitors an authentic, no-frills coastal experience rooted in history, nature, and fresh seafood.

Cortez isn't a town built for tourists—it's a town that lives its story every day. Stroll through its quiet streets and you'll pass century-old cottages where generations of fishermen have lived and worked. The Florida Maritime Museum, located in a historic schoolhouse, offers a deeper look at Cortez's seafaring past with exhibits on net-making, boat building, and the fishing industry that has sustained this community for more than a hundred years.

One of the biggest draws to Cortez is the food—you won't find chain restaurants here, but what you will find are some of the freshest seafood shacks and dockside dining spots around. Grab a table at a waterfront eatery and enjoy just-caught grouper, shrimp, oysters, or mullet while watching fishing boats return to the docks. For a true taste of the town's heritage, time your visit with the Cortez Commercial Fishing Festival held each February—an annual celebration of maritime culture featuring live music, seafood, and local art.

Outdoor Adventures and Coastal Beauty

Nature lovers will find plenty to do here as well. Launch a kayak or paddleboard into the bay to explore mangrove tunnels and quiet coves. You might spot dolphins, manatees, or a flock of roseate spoonbills skimming across the water. A short drive over the bridge brings you to Coquina Beach and Anna Maria Island, but Cortez itself has a quieter, more rustic charm that's perfect for a peaceful walk by the water or a lazy afternoon watching pelicans dive for fish.

Being a fishing village, it's no surprise that boat tours and charters are a big part of the Cortez experience. Local captains offer trips for everything from deep sea fishing to sunset cruises and eco tours through the nearby preserves. Whether you want to reel in a big catch or simply enjoy the breeze and salt air, getting out on the water is a must-do here.

Cortez isn't flashy—and that's exactly what makes it special. It's a place where the beauty is in the simplicity: a plate of fresh fish, a breeze off the bay, and the slow rhythm of a town that's been here, quietly doing its thing, for over a century. If you're craving an authentic Florida experience far from the crowds and full of soul, Cortez might just be the coastal treasure you didn't know you were looking for.

Cortez, Florida, and its surrounding areas offer a variety of activities for outdoor enthusiasts, including kayak rentals, bicycle rentals, and dog-friendly parks and beaches. Here are just a few—call or visit website for pricing and other information:

Water Sport Rentals

Kayak Jacks Paddlesports: A full-service mobile kayak and paddleboard rental company servicing Manatee County, including Bradenton, Anna Maria Island, and Longboat Key. Multiple launch sites.

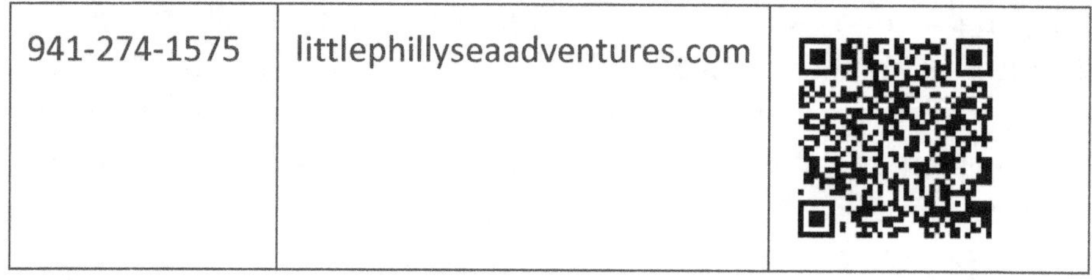

941-538-1448	kayak-jacks.com	

Little Philly Sea Adventures: Luxury boat rentals, jet ski rentals, fishing, rental packages.

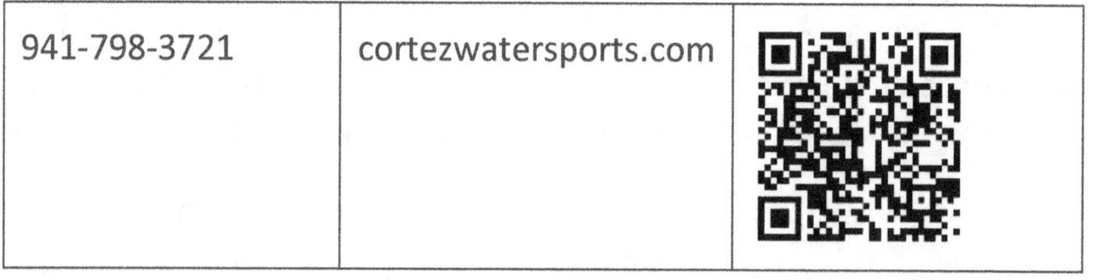

941-274-1575	littlephillyseaadventures.com	

Cortez Water Sports: Offers boat and jet ski rentals, providing opportunities for water-based adventures.

941-798-3721	cortezwatersports.com	

Boat Tours

Captain Kim's Boat Rides and Charters: Tours.

| 941-920-3307 | kimscharters.net | |

Captain Kathe *& First-Mate Pup-Pup Charters:* Tours.

| **941-812-3241** | captkathe.com | |

Bicycle Rentals

Beach Bums: offers bicycle, kayak, paddleboard, and golf cart rentals.

| 941-778-3316 | beachbumsami.com | |

Big Bam Bikes: ebike rentals.

| 941-240-1717 | bigbambikes.com | |

Dog-Friendly Parks and Beaches:

Palma Sola Causeway Park: 9000 Manatee Ave W, Bradenton, FL 34209

Located in Bradenton, this park is a sandy stretch popular for kayaking and picnicking. Leashed dogs are welcome to enjoy this pet-friendly shoreline.

Fort De Soto Park: Located in Tierra Verde, this park features a designated dog beach area where dogs can enjoy the water off-leash.

Please note that while dogs are welcome in many parks, they are generally not allowed on the beaches of Anna Maria Island.

Miami

Miami might be known for its beaches, Art Deco glam, and nightlife that goes till sunrise—but if you're looking to escape the buzz, you're in the right place. Just outside the city, there's a whole other Miami waiting to be discovered—one filled with quiet trails, tropical gardens, and wild, unforgettable experiences that have nothing to do with crowds or neon lights.

Want to walk among towering palms, exotic orchids, and plants from around the world? Tucked away in Coconut Grove, The Kampong offers a peaceful retreat in a tropical garden once home to legendary plant explorer Dr. David Fairchild. A little farther south, Deering Estate mixes history and nature with hiking trails, boardwalks through mangroves, and views of Biscayne Bay that make you forget you're anywhere near a city.

Craving some time in the wild? Shark Valley, just a short drive west into the Everglades, is the place to go. Bike or walk the 15-mile loop, or hop on the tram to see alligators, wading birds, and sweeping River of Grass views from the observation tower. It's flat, wide open, and feels like another planet—one where nature calls the shots.

If you've got kids (or are a kid at heart), Jungle Island delivers hands-on animal encounters, playful lemurs, and even a ropes course where you can zipline through the canopy. And if the kids want to cool off, Matheson Hammock Park has a shallow saltwater atoll pool that's perfect for splashing around. There's even a dog park if your pup is tagging along.

And of course, if you're into wildlife with feathers, fur, or scales, Flamingo Gardens is part zoo, part botanical sanctuary—with panthers, black bears, rescued birds of prey, and, yes, flamingos.

Miami isn't just one of Florida's busiest cities—it's also a gateway to some of the state's best natural escapes. So when you're ready to trade the traffic for trees or swap the beach scene for bird calls, adventure is just a short drive away.

Miami, Florida

Total day trip time: approximately 4-6 hours. 30-minute round-trip drive, leaving 3-5 ½ hours for fun and exploring.

Dogs: No

- **Fees:**
  - **General admission** (Includes Park, Nalu Acrobatic Show, Jungle Splash, Playground & Treewalk Village
    - $29.95 Child (ages 3-9)
    - $43.95 Adult (ages 10 and up)
    - Discounts for active military and family, veterans, first responders and their families, teachers and seniors. (must have ID proof)
  - **Treetop Trekking**:
    - $15.00-$99.00
    - $20.00 parking fee (covered garage)
- **Activities:** Wildlife viewing, acrobatic show, water playground, treewalk village, treetop trekking.

A Wild and Wonder-Filled Escape in the Heart of Miami

Located just across the causeway from downtown Miami on Watson Island, Jungle Island is a vibrant mix of wildlife, adventure, and immersive experiences—a place where nature and entertainment collide in colorful, unexpected ways. Originally known as Parrot Jungle when it opened in 1936, this beloved Miami attraction has evolved over the decades into a modern-day adventure park while still honoring its roots as a haven for exotic birds and rescued animals.

From the moment you enter, it's clear Jungle Island isn't your typical zoo. You'll encounter talkative parrots, playful lemurs, majestic sloths, capybaras, kangaroos, reptiles, and more—many of which you can meet up close during scheduled animal encounters or VIP experiences. Hand-feed flamingos, pose with a parrot perched on your shoulder, or even sign up to snuggle with a sloth (yes, it's as dreamy as it sounds).

But it's not just about the animals. Jungle Island has expanded to offer a range of active experiences for kids and adults alike. The Treewalk Village is a favorite for families, with rope bridges, treehouses, and climbing structures set in a shaded, tropical setting. Thrill-seekers can tackle the Skywire zipline, test their strength on the Ninja course, or cool off at SuperFlight, a wind tunnel that lets you experience the sensation of skydiving without ever leaving the ground.

Treetop Trekking at Jungle Island: Swing Through the Canopy in the Heart of Miami

Hidden beneath the towering palms and thick tropical foliage of Jungle Island, Treetop Trekking Miami offers an exhilarating adventure that lifts you high into the treetops—right in the middle of the city. This ropes and zipline course is perfect for visitors looking to challenge themselves, get active, and see Miami from a whole new angle.

The aerial adventure park features a variety of suspended bridges, tightropes, swinging logs, and thrilling ziplines that soar above the jungle canopy, with courses designed for both kids and adults. Whether you're a first-timer or an experienced climber, the course is built with multiple difficulty levels, so you can choose your own adventure at your own pace.

As you climb, swing, and zip from platform to platform, you'll be surrounded by the lush sounds of Jungle Island—birds calling in the distance, leaves rustling in the breeze, and maybe even a lemur watching from below. It's not just a workout for your body—it's a full-on sensory experience, and one of the most fun and unique ways to explore nature right in the middle of Miami.

Whether you're traveling with teens, friends, or your adventurous sidekick, Treetop Trekking is a must-try for thrill-seekers visiting Jungle Island.

For those who like their wild adventures a little more relaxed, there are shaded walking paths winding through lush landscaping, serene lagoons, and educational presentations that highlight the park's mission of animal conservation and care. Jungle Island also regularly hosts special events, from cultural festivals to kids' camps and seasonal celebrations.

Whether you're looking to connect with animals, let your kids run wild, or just escape the city bustle without leaving it behind, Jungle Island offers a playful blend of nature, adventure, and Miami flair. It's perfect for families, couples, or anyone who wants a day that's both exciting and just a little bit wild.

Hours	9:30 a.m.-5: p.m. daily
Phone	305-400-7000
Location	1111 Parrot Jungle Trail Miami, Florida 33132
Website	jungleisland.com

Suggested Supplies

Sunscreen	Bug repellant	Water shoes
Close-toed shoes (required for playground and treewalk village)	Stroller or wagon for children	Towels/change of clothes

Note: no outside food or beverages allowed

Coral Gables, Florida

Total day trip time: approximately 4 hours. 40-minute drive round trip, leaving 3+ hours for swimming/sunning.
Dogs: No
- **Fees: (Note:** no children under 3 years of age allowed)
    o $22.00 Adults (13 years and older)
    o $17.00 Child: (3 - 12 years)
- **Activities:** Swimming/sunning, picnicking (no coolers or glass allowed)

Swim in a Slice of History

Step into a tropical fantasy at Venetian Pool, one of the most unique and historic swimming spots in Florida. Tucked into the elegant neighborhood of Coral Gables, this iconic pool isn't just for cooling off—it's for stepping back in time. Built in 1924 from a coral rock quarry, the pool is fed by spring water and surrounded by Mediterranean-style architecture, complete with waterfalls, caves, a Venetian-style bridge, and palm-fringed loggias that feel like something out of a European postcard.

This isn't your average pool. It holds about 820,000 gallons of fresh spring water, which is drained and refilled daily during the busy season. The water is always refreshingly cool, making it the perfect retreat on a hot Florida day. The pool features shallow areas for lounging, deep swimming zones, and hidden grottos to explore—ideal for both casual swimmers and adventurous kids (note: children under 3 are not allowed in the pool for safety reasons).

There's also a shaded café area on-site if you want to grab a snack or cold drink, and plenty of room to relax, whether you're sunbathing by the water or sitting under a leafy canopy. If you're interested in the story behind the beauty, Venetian Pool offers glimpses into its colorful past with historic photos and architectural details that tell the tale of Coral Gables' development and George Merrick's vision for a Mediterranean-inspired community.

Whether you're visiting to swim, soak in the atmosphere, or snap photos of one of the most picturesque places in South Florida, Venetian Pool is a truly one-of-a-kind experience. It's part swimming hole, part historic landmark, and completely unforgettable.

Hours	Times vary; check the website
Phone	305-460-5306
Location	2701 De Soto Blvd, Coral Gables, FL 33134
Website	coralgables.com/attractions/venetian-pool

Suggested Supplies

Sunscreen	Towels	Sunglasses
Snacks/picnic supplies	Water/drinks	
Note: Umbrellas, coolers, alcohol and glass **not allowed**.		

Miami, Florida

Total day trip time: approximately 4 hours. 40-minute round-trip drive, leaving 3 hours 20 minutes for exploring nature.

Dogs: No

- **Fees:**
  - **Self Guided Tours**
    - $17.00-Adults Ages 18+
    - $12.00-Seniors 62 and older
    - $12.00-Students Must show valid student ID
    - $7.00-Children 6 -17 years old
    - $0-Young Children Three years and younger
  - **Guided Tours**
    - $27.00-Adults Ages 18+
    - $22.00-Seniors 62 and older
    - $22.00-Students Must show valid student ID
    - $12.00-Children 6 -17 years old
    - $0 -Young Children 3 years and younger

Note: Register by phone for admission waivers for Military Veterans (for card holder); Museums for All; Supplemental Nutrition Assistance Program (SNAP); and Women, Infants, and Children (WIC) recipients (with Electronic Benefit Transfer card)

- **Activities:** View unique and historical plants.

A Tropical Garden Escape in the Heart of Coconut Grove

Tucked away in the quiet, leafy neighborhood of Coconut Grove, The Kampong feels like a secret garden—lush, peaceful, and full of stories. Once the private home of famed horticulturist Dr. David Fairchild, this stunning tropical oasis now serves as a living museum, part of the National Tropical Botanical Garden, and one of the most beautiful, lesser-known day trips in South Florida.

Spread across nine serene acres along Biscayne Bay, The Kampong is a place where botanical science meets natural beauty. You won't find tidy flower beds or manicured lawns here. Instead, you'll wander beneath a canopy of towering palms, flowering trees, fruit-bearing plants, and exotic species from Southeast Asia, the Caribbean, Central and South America, and beyond. It's the kind of place where every path seems to hold a surprise—breadfruit trees, baobabs, vanilla orchids, or even rare bamboo species that Fairchild himself collected on his travels.

Walking the grounds feels like stepping into another world—one that's wild and curated at the same time. The historic Fairchild-Sweeney House, with its coral rock walls and breezy verandas, overlooks the bay and tells the story of a man who helped introduce hundreds of plants and fruits to the U.S. food supply. Though the house is not always open to the public, just seeing it framed by orchids and banyan trees adds to the atmosphere of a place shaped by passion and discovery.

Unlike more crowded gardens or parks, The Kampong offers quiet, slow-paced exploration, perfect for nature lovers, photographers, and those who simply need to recharge in a tranquil setting. Guided tours are available by appointment, but even a self-guided stroll through the trails invites reflection, inspiration, and awe at the diversity of plant life thriving just minutes from downtown Miami.

Whether you're interested in botany, history, or simply finding a little peace in the middle of the city, The Kampong is a hidden gem that invites you to pause, wander, and reconnect with the natural world.

Hours	Tuesday through Saturday, from 9:00 a.m. to 4:30 p.m. Last entry is 3:00 p.m. **NOTE: Book online** for exact times and to ensure entry due to limited parking.
Phone	305-442-7169
Location	4013 South Douglas Road Miami, FL
Website	ntbg.org/gardens/kampong

Suggested Supplies

Close-toed shoes (required)	Water (filling stations available)	Sunscreen
Bug repellant	Stroller or wagon for children	Binoculars

Miami, Florida

Total day trip time: approximately 5 hours. 1 hour drive round trip, leaving 4 hours for swimming, fun, and exploring.
Dogs: No/Yes (No dogs allowed at the swimming/marina park. Dogs are allowed at the west side where there is a 2 acre shaded dog park)

- **Fees:**
    o $6.00 per vehicle (up to 8 people), $4.00 single occupant
- **Activities:** swimming, hiking, dog park

Old Florida Charm by the Bay

Just south of Coral Gables, tucked along the edge of Biscayne Bay, Matheson Hammock Park feels like a throwback to a slower, gentler Florida. Shaded by swaying palms and ancient oaks, this 600-acre park offers a beautiful blend of natural coastal beauty, family-friendly recreation, and a touch of Miami history. With its quiet trails, scenic waterfront views, and laid-back atmosphere, it's the kind of place where both locals and visitors come to breathe a little deeper and enjoy a day outdoors—without the crowds.

At the heart of the park is its most unique feature: a man-made atoll pool, gently flushed by the tides of Biscayne Bay. This circular, saltwater swimming lagoon is perfect for children and families. It's shallow, calm, and ringed with soft sand—ideal for building sandcastles or watching little ones splash safely while sailboats drift by in the distance. For many Miami families, a visit to the atoll pool is a nostalgic rite of passage, passed down through generations.

But Matheson Hammock isn't just about relaxing by the water. The park also includes a shaded dog park, where your four-legged companion can romp and play off-leash. Nestled beneath the trees with space to roam, it's a favorite spot for locals who love to let their pups socialize and explore in a peaceful, natural setting.

The rest of the park offers plenty to discover. You can hike or bike through dense tropical hardwood hammock trails, take a walk along the seawall with bay views, or launch a kayak from the marina to explore the nearby mangroves. The historic coral rock buildings—built by the Civilian Conservation Corps in the 1930s—give the park a timeless charm, reminding visitors of the area's early efforts to preserve South Florida's unique natural beauty.

Whether you're swimming in the protected lagoon, watching the sunset over the bay, or letting your dog chase the breeze, Matheson Hammock Park is one of Miami's most peaceful and picturesque escapes—a little patch of paradise where the city melts away, and Old Florida lives on.

Hours	Park: Sunrise to sunset Office: 8 a.m. to 5 p.m.
Phone	305-665-5475
Location	9610 Old Cutler Road, Miami, FL 33156
Website	miamidade.gov/parks/matheson-hammock.asp

Suggested Supplies

Water	Snacks	Picnic supplies
Sunscreen	Beach blanket	Bug repellant
Waste pick-up bags for Fido	Sunglasses	Hiking boots/comfortable walking shoes
Swimwear	Towels	Beach shoes

Note: No flotation devices allowed.

Miami, Florida

Total day trip time: approximately 4 hours. 1-hour drive round trip, leaving 3 hours to explore the exhibits and ride a train.

Dogs: No

- **Fees:**
  - Admission
    - $12.00 Adult
    - $10.00 Child (Ages 3-12)
    - $0 Children 2 and under
    - $8.00 Seniors (65+)
    - BOGO AAA discount:
    - $0 Military:
    - $3.00 for up to 4 people: Museums4all (with EBT/WIC):
  - **Train ride** $10
- **Activities:** Historical train viewing, train ride, educational

A Presidential Ride Worth the Detour

Unlike most of the outdoor escapes and quiet nature spots in this book, the Gold Coast Railroad Museum earns its place for a different reason—it's simply too unique to leave out. For train enthusiasts and history buffs alike, this Miami museum offers a one-of-a-kind journey through the golden age of rail travel, anchored by one of the most remarkable artifacts of American transportation history: the Ferdinand Magellan, the presidential railcar used by Franklin D. Roosevelt, Harry Truman, Dwight Eisenhower, and Ronald Reagan.

This isn't just a look-but-don't-touch display. Visitors can step inside the same train car that carried U.S. presidents across the country during wartime and peace, see the custom features designed specifically for FDR—including bulletproof windows, armor-plated sides, and a wheelchair lift—and explore the intimate spaces where history was made, from a wood-paneled conference room to a private presidential suite.

The museum itself is located on the site of the former Naval Air Station Richmond, and houses over 40 historic railcars and engines, many of which are open to explore. The collection includes diesel locomotives, cabooses, freight cars, and beautifully restored passenger coaches. On weekends, you can even hop aboard a short train ride, perfect for families and anyone who wants to feel the click-clack of the rails beneath them.

Model train layouts, hands-on exhibits, and well-preserved memorabilia round out the experience, making this museum a hidden gem with heavyweight historical significance. Whether you're fascinated by the mechanics of rail travel or drawn to the legacy of American presidents, the Gold Coast Railroad Museum offers a rare and personal glimpse into a past where the train wasn't just a way to travel—it was a symbol of power, movement, and change.

In a book focused on Florida's quieter and lesser-known day trips, this unique stop might stand out—but for all the right reasons. It's a ride through history you won't forget.

Hours	Wednesday-Friday from 11:00 a.m. to 4:00 p.m. Saturday/Sunday 10:00 a.m.-4:00 p.m.
Phone	305-253-0063
Location	12450 SW 152nd Street Miami, FL 33177
Website	goldcoastrailroadmuseum.org

Suggested Supplies

Water	Stroller for children	Snacks

Miami, Florida

Total day trip time: approximately 4 ½ hours. 1 hour and 20-minute round-trip drive, leaving 3+ hours for watching and learning about monkeys.

Dogs: No

- **Fees:**
  - $20.00 (plus tax)Adults:
  - $10.00 (plus tax) Children (ages 3 - 9
    - Tours are available for additional fee.
- **Activities**: Primate viewing and education

Where Humans Are Caged and Monkeys Run Free

Tucked into the subtropical wilds of South Dade, Monkey Jungle flips the script on the traditional zoo experience. Here, humans walk through caged pathways, while monkeys roam freely through 30 acres of carefully preserved forest and habitat. It's not just a catchy slogan—it's an entirely different way of observing primates, and one of Florida's most unique day trip adventures.

Founded in 1935 as a research facility, Monkey Jungle has long focused on primate behavior, conservation, and education. Many of its residents—like the Java macaques—live in social groups in large, naturalistic environments. Watching them swing through the trees, forage for food, and interact with each other is a true joy, especially when you realize you're the one in the cage, safely tucked inside a wire-covered walkway that winds through their territory.

The park is home to over 300 primates, representing more than a dozen species, including chimpanzees, squirrel monkeys, howler monkeys, and the endangered golden-handed tamarin. One of the most memorable moments comes when the monkeys approach the mesh tunnels and visitors feed them through specially designed feeding buckets—an up-close, interactive experience that's as fun for adults as it is for kids.

In addition to watching the primates in their habitats, Monkey Jungle offers scheduled feeding sessions and narrated presentations, where you can learn about each species' social structure, intelligence, and conservation status. The park's commitment to primate care and scientific study makes it more than just entertainment—it's education in motion.

Whether you're an animal lover, a curious traveler, or a family looking for a fun, off-the-beaten-path outing, Monkey Jungle provides a rare chance to connect with incredible animals in an environment designed with their well-being in mind. It's Old Florida charm mixed with meaningful wildlife interaction, and it's unlike anything else you'll find in the state.

Hours	9:45 a.m. - 4:00 .pm.
Phone	305-235-1611
Location	14805 SW 216 St Miami, FL 33170
Website	monkeyjungle.com

Suggested Supplies

Comfortable walking shoes	Sunscreen	Bug repellant
Mask (if you choose a tour you must wear a mask when interacting with monkeys)	Stroller or wagon for children	Binoculars

Palmetto Bay, Florida

Total day trip time: approximately 1 hour. 20-minute drive round-trip, leaving 3+ hours for learning and exploration.

Dogs: No (ADA service dogs only)

- **Fees:**
  - $18.00 + tax adults (Ages 15+):
  - $16.00 + tax U.S. Active Duty Military:
  - $16.00 + tax U.S Honorably Discharged Veterans:
  - $16.00 + tax seniors (Ages 62+):
  - $10.00 + tax youth (4-14):
  - $0 ages 3 & under:
- **Activities:** Hiking, history, architecture, wildlife viewing, birdwatching

History, Hiking, and Untouched Florida Beauty

Nestled along the edge of Biscayne Bay in South Miami, the Deering Estate is a place where elegant history and wild nature meet. Once the private home of Charles Deering—an early 20th-century industrialist and art patron—this 450-acre preserve offers more than just a glimpse into Miami's past. It's also a living landscape, filled with native habitats, hiking trails, and archaeological treasures that make it one of the most enriching and unique day trips in South Florida.

At the heart of the estate are two beautifully preserved homes: the 1920s-era Stone House, with its thick limestone walls, secret wine cellar, and rooftop views, and the Richmond Cottage, which predates it as a former hotel turned family residence. Inside, visitors can explore museum-style exhibits that reflect Deering's interests in preservation, science, and the arts. The estate also hosts rotating art shows, lectures, and cultural events that bring its legacy into the present.

But beyond the architecture and art, the estate truly shines in its connection to Florida's natural environment. The grounds include coastal tropical hardwood hammocks, mangroves, salt marshes, and pine rocklands—rare ecosystems that once covered much of Miami but now survive in only a few protected areas. Miles of hiking trails wind through this landscape, offering quiet, shaded paths where visitors might spot deer, foxes, gopher tortoises, and over 170 species of birds.

For those looking for a deeper connection to the land, guided nature hikes and moonlit walking tours are offered seasonally, giving guests a chance to learn about native plants, archaeological sites, and the Tequesta people who lived here more than a thousand years ago. The estate is even home to one of the oldest burial mounds in Miami-Dade County, adding another layer to its rich and complex story.

Whether you're walking beneath a canopy of ancient trees, exploring the elegant halls of the Stone House, or watching the sun set over Biscayne Bay, Deering Estate offers a rare combination of culture, history, and raw natural beauty. It's a place that invites you to slow down, look closer, and appreciate both the wild and the refined sides of Florida's past.

Hours	10 a.m. – 5 p.m. (no admission after 4 p.m.)
Phone	305-680-5219
Location	16701 SW 72 Avenue, Palmetto Bay, Fl 33157
Website	deeringestate.org

Suggested Supplies

Sunscreen	Bug repellant	Hiking boots/comfortable walking shoes
Picnic supplies	Stroller or wagon for children	Binoculars
Water	Snacks	

Davie, Florida

Total day trip time: approximately 5 hours. 2-hour round-trip drive, leaving 3 hours for wildlife viewing and exploration.

Dogs: No

- **Fees:**
  - **General Admission**
    - $24.00 Adult (12+)
    - $17.00 Child (ages 3-11, 2 and under are free)
    - $19.20 Seniors (65+)
  - **Feed the Flamingos:** $55.00 per person
  - **Reptile encounter:** $55.00 adult/$35.00 children (11 and under)
- **Activities:** wildlife viewing, 60 acres of gardens

A Lush Escape into Florida's Wild Side

Step into a living postcard of Old Florida at Flamingo Gardens, a vibrant botanical garden and wildlife sanctuary located in Davie, just west of Fort Lauderdale. This 60-acre paradise feels like a tropical dream—home to towering trees, cascading orchids, and, of course, bright pink flamingos wading gracefully through quiet ponds. It's part garden, part zoo, part living history—and completely enchanting.

Originally founded in the 1920s, Flamingo Gardens is one of the oldest botanical gardens in South Florida, and it shows in the best way possible. The grounds are filled with massive champion trees, rare tropical and subtropical plants, butterfly and pollinator gardens, and shady paths that wind through exotic foliage. It's a place that invites you to slow down, wander, and soak in the beauty of South Florida's native landscape.

But the garden's heartbeat is its wildlife sanctuary, home to over 90 species of permanently injured or non-releasable native animals. Visitors can get an up-close look at Florida panthers, black bears, river otters, eagles, owls, alligators, and, yes, the iconic flamingos, which you can feed by hand. It's not a petting zoo—it's a space for education, conservation, and awe.

Take a narrated tram tour through the wetlands and citrus groves, explore the historic 1930s Wray Home Museum, or let the kids enjoy the aviary and wildlife presentations throughout the day. The blend of natural beauty, animal encounters, and peaceful walking trails makes Flamingo Gardens a perfect outing for all ages.

For those looking to connect with Florida's wild side—while surrounded by lush, tropical serenity—Flamingo Gardens is a magical retreat that leaves a lasting impression. Whether it's your first visit or your fifteenth, you'll walk away feeling like you've stepped into another world.

Hours	9:30 a.m.-5:00 p.m. daily (last entry at 4:00 p.m.)
Phone	954-473-2955
Location	3750 S Flamingo Rd, Davie, Fl 33330
Website	flamingogardens.org

Suggested Supplies

Sunscreen	Bug repellant	Stroller or wagon for kids
Binoculars	Comfortable walking shoes	

Note: No outside food or drinks! Food is available and is reasonably priced.

Coconut Creek

Total day trip time: approximately 5 hours. 2-hour drive round trip, leaving 3 hours for fun and exploring.
Dogs: No
- **Fees:**
  - $0
- **Activities:** hiking, biking, birdwatching, wildlife viewing

Description

Fern Forest Nature Center, located in Coconut Creek, Florida, is a 247-acre urban wilderness area renowned for its rich biodiversity and serene landscapes. The park is home to over 30 species of ferns, contributing to its name and making it a significant refuge for native flora and fauna.

Visitors can explore several well-maintained trails that meander through diverse ecosystems:

Cypress Creek Trail: A half-mile, wheelchair-accessible boardwalk that winds through a tropical hardwood forest and cypress-maple swamp, offering an immersive experience into the area's lush vegetation.

Prairie Overlook Trail: This one-mile loop traverses open prairie and oak forests, featuring an eight-foot observation platform that offers panoramic views of the preserve.

Red Maple Walk: A third-mile trail that delves into a red maple swamp; it's advisable to wear appropriate footwear, as the path can be wet and muddy.

The nature center also offers an Exhibit Hall with live displays of native reptiles, enhancing the educational experience for visitors. Additionally, amenities such as picnic areas, an amphitheater, and a sensory garden trail make it an ideal destination for both relaxation and learning.

Fern Forest Nature Center stands as a testament to conservation efforts, preserving a slice of Florida's natural heritage amidst urban development. It's a must-visit for nature enthusiasts and those seeking a tranquil escape.

Hours	9 a.m. to 5 p.m. daily
Phone	954-357-5198
Location	201 Lyons Rd South, Coconut Creek, Fl 33063
Website	broward.org/Parks/Pages/park.aspx?park=14

Suggested Supplies

Water	Snacks	Picnic supplies
Sunscreen	Bug repellant	Hiking boots/comfortable walking shoes
binoculars		

Miami, Florida

Total day trip time: approximately 6 hours. 3-hour round-trip drive, leaving 3 hours for exploring.

Dogs: No

- **Fees:**
  o $35.00 entrance fee per vehicle (7-day pass)
  o $30.00 per motorcycle (7-day pass)
  o $20.00 per pedestrian/cyclist/human-powered paddle-craft (7-day pass).
- **Activities:** walking, biking, tram ride, observation tower, wildlife viewing

Fifteen Miles of Wild Beauty and Open Sky

Deep in the northern reaches of Everglades National Park, far from the noise of the city, Shark Valley offers a stunning and surprisingly peaceful window into one of the most iconic landscapes in the world. Don't be fooled by the name—there are no sharks here. Instead, this vast, sawgrass-covered prairie teems with birds, turtles, and more alligators than you can count, basking along the trail or silently gliding through slow-moving water.

What makes Shark Valley special is how up-close and accessible it makes the Everglades feel. The main feature is a 15-mile loop trail, paved and flat, perfect for biking, walking, or riding the open-air tram that departs from the visitor center. As you travel the path, wildlife reveals itself gradually and constantly: roseate spoonbills flashing pink in the distance, anhinga drying their wings on the banks, or gators stretched out in the sun just feet away. It's the kind of place where you don't need binoculars—nature is right there beside you.

About halfway through the loop, the trail leads to an observation tower, offering a sweeping, 360-degree view over the endless "River of Grass." From this gentle rise, the subtle textures and colors of the Everglades come alive—glittering water, rustling reeds, and distant birds riding the thermals. It's quiet up there, and humbling, a reminder of just how vast and wild this protected land remains.

If you're not up for the full loop on foot or bike, the Shark Valley Tram Tour is a great option. Naturalist guides offer insight into the ecology, history, and preservation of the park, making it ideal for first-time visitors or those who want to learn while taking in the scenery.

The Shark Valley Visitor Center is small but informative, with maps, exhibits, and rangers available to answer questions or offer tips on what to look for during your adventure. Bring water, sunscreen, and a camera—this is the kind of place where even a short stroll can feel like stepping into a National Geographic documentary.

Shark Valley isn't flashy, and it doesn't need to be. It's wild, beautiful, and exactly what you imagine when you picture the Everglades—an ancient, living landscape where nature calls the shots and time seems to slow to the rhythm of the water. Whether you bike it, walk it, or ride the tram, this is one of South Florida's most unforgettable day trips.

Hours	• Entrance: 8:30 a.m. to 6:00 p.m. • Visitor Center: 9:00 a.m. to 5:00 p.m. • Shark Valley Tram Tours 8:30 a.m. to 6:00 p.m.
Location	36000 SW 8th Street Miami, Florida 33194
Website	nps.gov/ever/planyourvisit/svdirections.htm

Suggested Supplies

Water	Snacks	Sunscreen
Sunhat	Bug repellant	Binoculars

Beyond the Map: Why These Coasts Deserve a Detour

While the majority of adventures in this book are within a 2 to 2½ hour drive of Florida's major cities, there are two coastal regions that deserve a spotlight of their own—the Lee Island Coast on the Gulf and the Treasure Coast on the Atlantic.

They don't quite fit the geographic parameters of the rest of this guide, but they *do* fit the spirit of it perfectly. These are places where Old Florida still lingers in the salty air, where nature leads the way, and where quiet trails, peaceful beaches, and small-town charm are easy to find.

So if you're planning a long weekend, passing through on a road trip, or just feel like wandering a little farther, these two regions are worth the extra miles. What you'll find there is what this book is all about—a slower pace, fewer crowds, and a deeper connection to Florida's wild, beautiful heart.

Coastal Contrast: The Lee Island & Treasure Coasts

Though separated by the width of the state, the Lee Island Coast and Treasure Coast share a common thread: both are home to natural beauty, laid-back living, and local charm that has resisted overdevelopment.

The Lee Island Coast, tucked along Florida's southwest Gulf shoreline, is a world of sugar-white sands, island hopping, and warm, shallow bays. It includes places like Sanibel, Captiva, and Cayo Costa, where shells outnumber souvenir shops and sea turtles outnumber sunbathers.

On the opposite shore, the Treasure Coast stretches along the Atlantic, from Sebastian to Hobe Sound, offering quiet beach towns, mangrove estuaries, and history-rich communities. This coast got its name from the Spanish treasure fleets that sank offshore, but for today's traveler, the real treasure lies in its peaceful nature preserves, local art, and coastal hikes.

In the pages ahead, you'll find a quick overview of the well-loved destinations in each region—followed by a deeper dive into the lesser-known spots that are just waiting to be discovered.

Along Florida's southwest Gulf shoreline, west of Fort Myers, the **Lee Island Coast** offers a quieter kind of beauty. This region is known for its soft white sands, warm Gulf waters, and an easygoing pace that stands in contrast to the busier coastal destinations of the state. Made up of barrier islands, nature preserves, and small towns with big character, the Lee Island Coast captures the spirit of Old Florida—where natural landscapes take center stage and life slows down just enough to let you breathe it all in.

The area is perfect for those who want to swap crowds for coastline, trading theme parks and high-rises for wildlife viewing, shell-strewn beaches, mangrove estuaries, and small-town charm. Whether you're here to paddle, walk, birdwatch, or just sit and listen to the waves, this stretch of coast offers something special.

Here are a few of the region's best-known highlights:

Sanibel Island – Famous for being one of the best shelling destinations in the world, Sanibel's unique east-west orientation means the Gulf washes thousands of seashells onto its shores daily. You won't find high-rises or fast-food chains here—just bike paths, cozy cottages, and the quiet rustle of palms. It's a haven for families, nature lovers, and anyone who wants to unwind.

Captiva Island – Just north of Sanibel and connected by a small bridge, Captiva is known for its vibrant colors, quaint charm, and incredible sunsets. It's a great place for a romantic day trip, with art galleries, beachside restaurants, and dolphin-watching cruises.

Lovers Key State Park – Between Fort Myers Beach and Bonita Springs, Lovers Key offers an escape into Florida's coastal wilderness. With boardwalk trails, unspoiled beaches, and calm waterways for kayaking, it's a peaceful spot for both relaxation and adventure.

J.N. "Ding" Darling National Wildlife Refuge – This Sanibel refuge is one of the best places in the state to view wildlife in its natural habitat. Visitors often spot alligators, roseate spoonbills, otters, and raccoons while exploring by car, bike, or kayak. It's a top spot for birdwatchers and photographers.

Edison & Ford Winter Estates (Fort Myers) – Step back in time with a visit to the historic homes and gardens of Thomas Edison and Henry Ford. Set along the Caloosahatchee River, the estates offer a look into the inventors' winter lives and feature a museum, botanical gardens, and preserved laboratories.

These highlights offer a taste of the Lee Island Coast's charm—but there's so much more to discover just off the beaten path. In the next section, we'll explore the **lesser-known gems** of this coastline—places where nature still leads the way, and peace and quiet are easy to find.

Hidden Gems of the Lee Island Coast

While Sanibel and Captiva may steal the spotlight, some of the most rewarding day trips on the Lee Island Coast are tucked just beyond the usual routes. These lesser-known spots offer a deeper connection to nature and Old Florida charm—without the traffic or the crowds.

Whether you're reaching a remote beach by ferry, exploring mangrove-lined estuaries, or strolling through a historic fishing village, each of these destinations invites you to slow down and see another side of Southwest Florida. These places aren't usually found in glossy travel brochures—but they're unforgettable once discovered.

Cayo Costa State Park

Address: Cayo Costa State Park, 4 Nautical Miles West of Pine Island, Boca Grande, FL
Access: By ferry from Pine Island (via Captiva Cruises or private boat)

Cayo Costa is one of the last truly undeveloped barrier islands in Florida. Accessible only by boat or ferry, the park features nine miles of untouched shoreline, hiking trails, and some of the best shelling in the state. There are no restaurants or cars—just dunes, driftwood, wildlife, and quiet.

- **Activities:** Shelling, hiking, swimming, wildlife viewing, paddling, primitive camping
- **Dog Policy:** Allowed on leash, but not on the beach
- **Tip:** Bring everything you need—including water and snacks. There are no concessions.

North Captiva Island

Address for ferry departure: Island Girl Charters, 16498 Captiva Dr, Captiva, FL 33924
Access: By ferry, water taxi, or private boat

Separated from Captiva by Redfish Pass, North Captiva is a quiet, residential island with no cars—just golf carts and sandy paths. The beaches are beautiful and rarely crowded, making it ideal for a relaxing day trip. You'll need to plan ahead, but the reward is worth it.

- **Activities:** Beachcombing, swimming, sunset watching, shelling
- **Dog Policy:** Varies by property and access point—check in advance
- **Tip:** Rentals and access may require coordination, so this is best for travelers who enjoy planning ahead or booking with a local host.

Bunche Beach Preserve

Address: 18201 John Morris Rd, Fort Myers, FL 33908

Located between Sanibel Causeway and Fort Myers Beach, this preserve is a hidden pocket of coastal habitat. Bunche Beach is ideal for low-tide walks, birdwatching, and peaceful kayaking. The preserve's shallow waters and mudflats attract wading birds, crabs, and all kinds of coastal wildlife.

- **Activities:** Birdwatching, kayaking, paddleboarding, photography
- **Dog Policy:** Dogs allowed on leash
- **Tip:** Visit during low tide for the best birding. Bring water shoes—shorelines can be muddy.

Matlacha & Pine Island

Central location for visitor info: 4577 Pine Island Rd NW, Matlacha, FL 33993

Matlacha is a funky, colorful village filled with art galleries, seafood shacks, and canal-side cottages. It leads to Pine Island—Florida's largest Gulf Coast island—which feels more like rural farmland than a beach town. It's great for cycling, kayaking, and finding hidden spots to fish or picnic.

- **Activities:** Fishing, kayaking, art galleries, local food, cycling
- **Dog Policy:** Leashed pets welcome in outdoor areas and along docks
- **Tip:** Don't miss the local art co-ops or a walk down the Calusa Heritage Trail near Pineland

Lovers Key State Park

Address: 8700 Estero Blvd, Bonita Springs, FL 34134

Though technically better known, Lovers Key still feels like a hidden treasure—especially if you go early in the morning. It offers serene beaches, shaded hiking and biking trails, and kayak rentals for paddling through mangrove-lined estuaries. The Black Island Trail offers a quiet route for birding and wildlife spotting.

- **Activities:** Kayaking, hiking, swimming, shelling, wildlife viewing
- **Dog Policy:** Dogs allowed on leash in most areas, but not on the beach
- **Tip:** Parking fills quickly on weekends—go early or visit on a weekday for a quieter experience

The Treasure Coast: Old Florida Vibes, Uncrowded Shores

Where Florida's Quiet Coastline Meets Hidden History

Located along Florida's southeastern Atlantic shoreline, the Treasure Coast stretches from Sebastian to Hobe Sound, encompassing parts of Indian River, St. Lucie, and Martin counties. This region got its name from the Spanish treasure fleets that sank offshore in the 1700s—but today's "treasure" lies more in its quiet charm, pristine nature, and laid-back pace than in sunken gold.

Less developed than its southern neighbors in Palm Beach and Miami-Dade, the Treasure Coast offers miles of unspoiled beaches, coastal trails, estuarine preserves, and small towns with real character. You won't find high-rise resorts lining every inch of shoreline here. Instead, you'll find local cafes, art walks, and nature centers nestled in between beaches and wetlands.

This is a great region for paddling, hiking, birding, or just relaxing by the ocean without the crowds. Popular stops like Vero Beach, Fort Pierce, and Stuart offer a blend of culture and coastline, while local parks and preserves give you easy access to wild Florida.

Here are a few of the region's more well-known highlights:

Vero Beach – A charming coastal town with a walkable downtown, scenic beaches, and a small but thriving arts scene. Perfect for a day of beachcombing followed by lunch at a local café.

Fort Pierce Inlet State Park – Known for its excellent snorkeling, fishing, and paddling opportunities, this park offers easy access to both the Atlantic and the Indian River Lagoon.

Blowing Rocks Preserve (Jupiter Island) – A dramatic stretch of shoreline where limestone formations send ocean spray high into the air during rough seas—one of the most unique coastal sights in the state.

Hobe Sound Beach – One of the most peaceful beaches on the Atlantic, great for walking, shelling, and simply soaking up the sound of the surf.

While these are wonderful places to explore, the real charm of the Treasure Coast lies in the spots you won't hear much about. In the next section, we'll dive into some of those hidden gems—off-the-radar preserves, quiet trails, and low-key adventures that feel worlds away from Florida's busier shores.

Hidden Gems of the Treasure Coast

While the main towns of the Treasure Coast are lovely in their own right, this stretch of Florida coastline is also home to quiet preserves, shady boardwalks, and remote beaches where it's still possible to enjoy the sound of the waves without a crowd.

These destinations are perfect for day trippers who want to slip off the main road and into the Florida few people take the time to see. Whether you're walking under a canopy of oaks, spotting manatees in the lagoon, or kayaking through mangroves, you'll find a more peaceful, natural side of the coast here.

Indrio Savannahs Preserve

Address: 5275 Tozour Rd, Fort Pierce, FL 34951

Located just inland from the Indian River Lagoon, Indrio Savannahs is a quiet preserve with several miles of looped hiking trails that wind through pine flatwoods and marshy savannahs. Wildlife is plentiful— look for sandhill cranes, gopher tortoises, and otters along the edges of the wetlands.

- **Activities:** Hiking, birding, photography, wildlife observation
- **Dog Policy:** Dogs allowed on leash
- **Tip:** Trails can be soggy after rain—wear sturdy shoes or boots.

Spruce Bluff Preserve

Address: 611 Dar Ln, Port St. Lucie, FL 34984

A hidden slice of history and wilderness tucked along the St. Lucie River. The preserve has two short trails—one leads to a high bluff with views of the river, while the other winds past a pioneer cemetery and the site of a 19th-century settlement. It's a peaceful place for quiet reflection or a short nature walk.

- **Activities:** Hiking, photography, birdwatching, historic markers
- **Dog Policy:** Leashed pets allowed
- **Tip:** Stop at nearby Veterans Park at Rivergate for kayak rentals and additional river access.

Savannas Preserve State Park (Environmental Education Center Trailhead)

Address: 2541 SE Walton Rd, Port St. Lucie, FL 34952

This is one of the largest freshwater marsh systems along Florida's east coast. Visitors can explore via a network of hiking trails, boardwalks, and waterways. The education center trailhead is a great place to start, with interpretive signage, accessible paths, and options for both short and longer walks.

- **Activities:** Hiking, wildlife viewing, paddling (from nearby launches), educational exhibits
- **Dog Policy:** Dogs allowed on leash
- **Tip:** This is a good spot for a quiet morning walk before heading to nearby beaches.

Bear Point Sanctuary

Address: 2601 S Ocean Dr, Fort Pierce, FL 34949

Overlooking the Indian River Lagoon, Bear Point is a small, lesser-known sanctuary with shaded walking trails, observation decks, and excellent opportunities to spot dolphins and manatees.

- **Activities:** Walking, manatee viewing, fishing, birdwatching
- **Dog Policy:** Dogs allowed on leash
- **Tip:** Bring binoculars and take the boardwalk out to the water's edge—it's one of the area's best-kept secrets.

Jensen Beach to Jupiter Inlet Aquatic Preserve

Access Points Vary – Best Entry: Jensen Beach Causeway Park, 4191 NE Ocean Blvd, Jensen Beach, FL 34957

This massive protected waterway hugs the barrier islands along the Treasure Coast. While much of it is only accessible by water, several parks and boat launches allow visitors to paddle through mangroves, explore spoil islands, and observe wildlife. Calm, clear waters make this ideal for beginner paddlers.

- **Activities:** Kayaking, paddleboarding, swimming, birdwatching
- **Dog Policy:** Leashed pets welcome at most access points, but not on all islands
- **Tip:** Check wind conditions before heading out—mornings are typically calmer

The Treasure Coast may not always make the top of the Florida travel brochures, but that's exactly what makes it so special. This stretch of coastline offers a rare blend of quiet beaches, wildlife-rich estuaries, shaded nature trails, and small towns that still feel deeply connected to Old Florida.

And while nature is the star here, the region also carries a deep sense of history—especially offshore. In the early 1700s, a fleet of Spanish treasure ships sank just off this coast during a hurricane, scattering gold, silver, and jewels across the sea floor. The area takes its name from that story, and you can explore it in depth at the **Mel Fisher's Treasure Museum** in Sebastian. This small but fascinating stop showcases recovered shipwreck artifacts, Spanish coins, and the story of one man's quest to bring history to the surface. It's a great add-on to any coastal day trip.

Whether you're paddling through mangroves, walking a boardwalk, or just sitting on a quiet beach, the Treasure Coast is the kind of place that invites you to slow down and reconnect—with Florida, and with yourself.

It's not flashy. It's not crowded. It's just quietly unforgettable.

Conclusion

The Florida You Remember—And Can Still Find

If you've made it this far, chances are you feel the same way I do—that Florida is more than just theme parks, traffic, and high-rises. It's still the place where the breeze carries the scent of salt, where herons stand watch in the shallows, and where a quiet dirt road might just lead you to your new favorite place.

When I was growing up in Sarasota in the 1960s, it wasn't hard to find solitude. You could take a slow drive with the windows down, follow the curve of the Gulf, and stumble across a sleepy fishing village, an empty beach, or a hammock draped in Spanish moss. It felt wild. It felt untouched. And even though Florida has changed, I promise you— those places still exist.

You just have to know where to look.

This book was written to help you do just that: to help you step off the beaten path and find the quiet, soulful corners of Florida that don't show up in brochures. Maybe you're a local hoping for a breath of fresh air close to home, or maybe you're a visitor who doesn't want the same experience as everyone else. Either way, the Florida you're looking for—the one that speaks in birdsong, crashing waves, and cicada hums—is still out there.

And you don't need weeks of planning to find it. All it takes is a free afternoon, a good map, and a little curiosity.

Each trip in this book was chosen because it offers something simple, beautiful, and grounded—a chance to reconnect with nature, with the past, or maybe just with yourself. Whether you're paddling a spring-fed river, biking a trail through an ancient forest, or walking the quiet streets of an old coastal town, I hope you felt something familiar... a kind of peace that's harder to find these days, but never out of reach.

So pack your "picnic pack," bring the dog if the trail allows it, keep that old map folded in the glove box, and don't rush. Let the road take you somewhere unexpected. Let Florida surprise you again.

Because the real Florida—the one we remember, the one worth finding—is still here.

And now, you know the way.

Enjoyed the Journey? Leave a Review!

If *Florida Day Trip Adventures* helped you discover a new favorite place—or simply reminded you of why you love this beautiful state—I'd be so grateful if you'd take a moment to leave a review.

Your feedback doesn't just help me—it helps others, too. Honest reviews help readers decide if this guide is right for them, and every review (even just a few words!) helps boost the book's visibility so more people can find and enjoy Florida's quieter, lesser-known treasures.

So if you found a hidden trail, a peaceful spring, or just enjoyed flipping through the pages and dreaming of your next day trip, I'd love to hear from you.

Use your phone camera to scan the QR code or go to your Amazon account to review this book. I would love an honest review of what you thought of the book.

Thank you for coming along on the adventure—and for helping others discover the joy of spontaneous, well-planned fun in the Sunshine State.

—Janice Pilson

References

Admin, B. D. (n.d.). *Two Tails Ranch | All About Elephants Williston, Florida near Gainesville | Asian and African Elephants.* https://allaboutelephants.com/

Alfred B. Maclay Gardens State Park. (n.d.). Florida State Parks. https://www.floridastateparks.org/index.php/MaclayGardens/

Animal petting area, children's parties, event venue, park | HorsePower for Kids | Tampa. (n.d.). HorsePower for Kids. https://www.horsepowerforkids.com/

Arcadia Mill Archaeological Site | Historic Pensacola. (n.d.). https://historicpensacola.org/explore-arcadia-mill/hours-tickets/arcadia-mill-archaeological-site/

Arcadia Mill Archaeological Site | Historic Pensacola. (n.d.). https://historicpensacola.org/explore-arcadia-mill/hours-tickets/arcadia-mill-archaeological-site/

Beach Bums. (2022, July 19). *Bicycle rentals, kayak rentals, golf cart rental | Beach bums.* Beach Bums Island Attitude. https://beachbumsami.com/

Big Bam Bikes. (2024, December 15). *Big Bam eBikes | ebike sales and rentals in Venice Florida.* Big Bam eBikes | Ebike Sales | 941-240-1717 | 412 E. Venice Ave. Venice, FL 34285. https://bigbambikes.com/

Big Lagoon State Park. (n.d.). Florida State Parks. https://www.floridastateparks.org/BigLagoon

Big Talbot Island State Park. (n.d.). Florida State Parks. https://www.floridastateparks.org/parks-and-trails/big-talbot-island-state-park

Big Talbot Island State Park. (n.d.). Florida State Parks. https://www.floridastateparks.org/parks-and-trails/big-talbot-island-state-park

Blackwater River State Park. (n.d.). Florida State Parks. https://www.floridastateparks.org/parks-and-trails/blackwater-river-state-park

Boat rentals, jet ski rentals, paddle board rentals, kayak rentals, vacation rentals - Anna Maria Island, FL. (n.d.). https://www.littlephillyseaadventures.com/

Boat rentals, jet ski rentals, paddle board rentals, kayak rentals, vacation rentals - Anna Maria Island, FL. (n.d.). https://www.littlephillyseaadventures.com/

Bruno, K. (2025, March 6). *Adventure Landing & Shipwreck Island Water Park | Jacksonville Beach, FL*. Jacksonville Beach. https://jacksonville-beach.adventurelanding.com/

Captain Kathe. (n.d.). https://captkathe.com/

Carson Springs Wildlife Conservation Foundation. (n.d.). *Carson Springs Wildlife Conservation Foundation*. https://www.carsonspringswildlife.org/

Charters, K. (n.d.). *Kim's Charters*. Kim's Charters. https://kimscharters.net/

Chase-n-Fins. (n.d.). *Chase-n-Fins*. https://chase-n-fins.com/

Cruises — Laguna's Beach Bar + grill. (n.d.). Laguna's Beach Bar + Grill. https://lagunaspensacolabeach.com/dolphin-cruise

De Leon Springs State Park. (n.d.). Florida State Parks. https://www.floridastateparks.org/parks-and-trails/de-leon-springs-state-park

Deering Estate. (2025, February 4). *Our mission of Florida Nature Preserve & Conservation efforts | Deering Estate*. https://deeringestate.org/about/conservation/

Devil's Millhopper Geological State Park. (n.d.). Florida State Parks. https://www.floridastateparks.org/parks-and-trails/devils-millhopper-geological-state-park

Discover Gainesville: Stay for adventure. (2025, January 13). Visit Gainesville. https://www.visitgainesville.com/

ECOmersion. (2025, March 9). *Ecomersion - Ecomersion Connecting People with Nature.* Ecomersion. https://ecomersion.com/

Edward Ball Wakulla Springs State Park. (n.d.). Florida State Parks. https://www.floridastateparks.org/WakullaSprings

Escape Room Tampa| Can you escape? (2025, January 7). Escape Room Tampa, Florida | Can You Escape? https://can-you-escape.com/

Eureka Springs Conservation Park. (n.d.). Hillsborough County, FL. https://hcfl.gov/locations/eureka-springs-conservation-park

Exploring Pensacola Beach with Your Dog: Our Pet-Friendly Guide - Pensacola Beach Property. (n.d.). https://www.pensacolabeachproperty.com/blog/pensacola-beach-dog-friendly-guide

Eye, O. (n.d.). *The Orlando Eye at ICON Park - Orlando Attractions & Entertainment.* The Orlando Eye. https://www.theorlandoeye.com/

Family Farm | Aunt Louise's Farm | United States. (n.d.). Aunt Louise's Farm. https://www.auntlouisesfarm.com/

Fern Forest Nature Center. (n.d.). https://www.broward.org/Parks/Pages/park.aspx?park=14

FLORIDA | Dinosaur World. (n.d.). Dinosaur World. https://www.dinosaurworld.com/florida

Florida Caverns State Park. (n.d.). Florida State Parks. https://www.floridastateparks.org/parks-and-trails/florida-caverns-state-park

Florida Tours, Manatee and Dolphin, Bioluminescence, Orlando Biking – BK Adventure. (2025, January 15). *FLBREAK-Promo-.* https://www.bkadventure.com/

Florida Tours, Manatee and Dolphin, Bioluminescence, Orlando Biking
– BK Adventure. (2025, January 15). *FLBREAK-Promo-*.
https://www.bkadventure.com/

Frisky Mermaid Dolphin Cruises & Pontoon Boat Rentals. (n.d.). *Frisky
Mermaid Dolphin Cruises & Pontoon Boat Rentals.*
https://www.friskyboattours.com/

GETPaul. (2020, May 8). *Catty Shack Ranch Wildlife Sanctuary.* Catty
Shack Ranch. https://cattyshack.org/

Gold Coast Railroad Museum | Miami. (n.d.). GCRM.
https://www.goldcoastrailroadmuseum.org/

Home - Tallahassee Museum. (2025, January 7). Tallahassee Museum.
https://tallahasseemuseum.org/

Ichetucknee Springs State Park. (n.d.). Florida State Parks.
https://www.floridastateparks.org/parks-and-trails/ichetucknee-
springs-state-park

Jolly Roger Beach Shop on St. George Island Florida. (n.d.).
https://jollyrogersgi.com/

Jolly Sailing. (n.d.). *Jolly sailing.* https://jollysailing.com/

Jungle Island. (2025, March 21). *Jungle Island - Animal Interactions &
Exhibits - Fun Miami FL Attractions.* https://www.jungleisland.com/

Kayak Jacks. (2024, April 8). *Home page - Kayak Jacks.* https://kayak-
jacks.com/

Lake Jackson Mounds Archaeological State Park. (n.d.). Florida State
Parks. https://www.floridastateparks.org/parks-and-trails/lake-
jackson-mounds-archaeological-state-park

Lettuce Lake Park. (n.d.). Hillsborough County, FL.
https://hcfl.gov/locations/lettuce-lake-conservation-park

Leu Gardens. (n.d.). https://www.leugardens.org/Home

Merritt Island National Wildlife Refuge | U.S. Fish & Wildlife Service. (2019, March 1). FWS.gov. https://www.fws.gov/refuge/merritt-island

Miami-Dade County Online Services. (n.d.). *Matheson Hammock Park - Miami-Dade County.* https://www.miamidade.gov/parks/matheson-hammock.asp

Mike Roess Gold Head Branch State Park. (n.d.). Florida State Parks. https://www.floridastateparks.org/parks-and-trails/mike-roess-gold-head-branch-state-park

Morningside Nature Center. (n.d.). https://www.gainesvillefl.gov/Parks/Morningside-Nature-Center

National Tropical Botanical Garden. (2025, March 18). *The Kampong - National Tropical Botanical Garden.* https://ntbg.org/gardens/kampong/

Official Travel Website for Jacksonville FL - Visit Jacksonville. (n.d.). *Official travel website for Jacksonville FL - Visit Jacksonville.* Visit Jacksonville. https://www.visitjacksonville.com/?utm_source=google&utm_medium=ppc&utm_campaign=madden%20aor-flvj&utm_content=leisure_sem&gad_source=1&gclid=CjOKCQjwy46_BhDOARIsAIvmcwOaH8qVRe64ceNneDyEMAQoRdB9AOO6NJs1Z7Z2PyrnNq8X-4JeW_4aAqqXEALw_wcB

Okefenokee National Wildlife Refuge | U.S. Fish & Wildlife Service. (n.d.). FWS.gov. https://www.fws.gov/refuge/okefenokee

Orlando Tree Trek Adventure Park | Orlando, Florida's #1 outdoor ropes course adventure. (2023, May 5). Orlando Tree Trek. https://www.orlandotreetrek.com/

Orlando Trip Planning | Visitor Guides, maps & vacation ideas. (n.d.).
https://www.visitorlando.com/plan/?utm_source=google&utm_medi
um=cpc-nbr&utm_campaign=us-in-state-sess-h1-
2025&utm_content=prospects&utm_partner=icon&adara_campaigni
d=15560477031&adara_pixelid=431759&gad_source=1&gclid=CjOKC
Qjwy46_BhDOARIsAIvmcwMr43Rn9ESOEBLlg5esez-
GLD0DGG8DYMCmrUeS_TLvMeK8rHzenxMaAu2PEALw_wcB&gclsrc=
aw.ds

Paynes Prairie Preserve State Park. (n.d.). Florida State Parks.
https://www.floridastateparks.org/parks-and-trails/paynes-prairie-
preserve-state-park

Pinellas County Florida - Weedon Island Preserve. (n.d.).
https://www.weedonislandpreserve.org/

Pinellas County Government. (2025, March 12). *Fort de Soto Park -
Pinellas County*. Pinellas County. https://pinellas.gov/parks/fort-de-
soto-park

Premier Dolphin Cruise. (n.d.). Premier Dolphin Cruise.
https://www.pensacoladolphincruise.com/

San Felasco Hammock Preserve State Park. (n.d.). Florida State Parks.
https://www.floridastateparks.org/parks-and-trails/san-felasco-
hammock-preserve-state-park

Santa Fe College Teaching Zoo | Gainesville Florida. (n.d.). Santa Fe
College. https://www.sfcollege.edu/zoo/

Scenic Boat Tour. (2013, May 16). *Scenic Boat Tour | Winter Park
Florida | Boat ride | Chain of Lakes*. Scenic Boat Tour | a Winter Park
Tradition. https://www.scenicboattours.com/

Shank, J. (2025, March 20). *Home - Flamingo Gardens*. Flamingo
Gardens. https://flamingogardens.org/

*Shark Valley Visitor Center - Everglades National Park (U.S. National
Park Service)*. (n.d.).
https://www.nps.gov/ever/planyourvisit/svdirections.htm

Shingle Creek Regional Park. (n.d.). Osceola County. https://www.osceola.org/Community/Parks-and-Conservation-Lands/Find-a-Park-Facility-or-Conservation-Area/Shingle-Creek-Regional-Park

Silver Springs State Park – world famous glass bottom boats. (n.d.). https://silversprings.com/

Skydive the Gulf | Skydiving Pensacola & Gulf Shores, AL. (2023, November 29). Skydive the Gulf. https://www.skydivethegulf.com/

St Marks Headwaters Greenway - Park Index. (n.d.). https://cms.leoncountyfl.gov/Government/Departments/Resource-Stewardship/Parks-Recreation/Park-Index?park-id=14178

St. George Island Beach Gear Rentals - VayK Gear. (2025, March 11). VayK Gear. https://vaykgear.com/st-george-island/

St. Johns River Water Management District. (2024, November 26). *Lake Apopka North Shore – SJRWMD*. SJRWMD. https://www.sjrwmd.com/lands/recreation/lake-apopka/

St. Marks National Wildlife Refuge | U.S. Fish & Wildlife Service. (2024, July 1). FWS.gov. https://www.fws.gov/refuge/st-marks

Sunken Gardens. (n.d.). https://sunkengardens.org/

Tampa Bay Fun Boat. (n.d.). *Tampa Bay's #1 party boat tours and cruises - Tampa Bay Fun Boat*. https://tampabayfunboat.com/

Tarkiln Bayou Preserve State Park. (n.d.). Florida State Parks. https://www.floridastateparks.org/parks-and-trails/tarkiln-bayou-preserve-state-park

The city of Tallahassee. (n.d.). https://www.talgov.com/parks/parks-cascades

Timucuan Ecological & Historic Preserve (U.S. National Park Service). (n.d.). https://www.nps.gov/timu/index.htm

Timucuan Parks Foundation. (2022, September 1). *Kathryn Abbey Hanna Park - Timucuan Parks Foundation*. https://www.timucuanparks.org/parks/kathryn-abbey-hanna-park/

Timucuan Parks Foundation. (2024, December 11). *7 Creeks Recreation Area – Jacksonville - Timucuan Parks Foundation*. https://www.timucuanparks.org/7-creeks-jax/

Venetian Pool | Coral Gables. (n.d.). https://www.coralgables.com/attractions/venetian-pool

Visit Miami. (2022, October 31). Visit Miami | Hotel and Visitor Information. https://visitmiami.com/

Visit Tallahassee. (2025, March 26). *Info, Events & Things to do in Tallahassee | Visit Tallahassee*. https://visittallahassee.com/

Visit Tampa Bay. (n.d.). https://www.visittampabay.com/?gad_source=1&gclid=CjwKCAjw7p O_BhAlEiwA4pMQvLqtOATENyG9KXPTLtrS1v0L7np8QuXLzBpYVLr57S NPnU14qpBvqBoCpnwQAvD_BwE

Wacissa River Canoe & Kayak Rentals & Airboat Tours. (n.d.). http://www.wacissarivercanoerentals.com/

Wdd. (n.d.). *Gatorland*. https://www.gatorland.com/

Wildlife Park, Zoo, animal attractions | Miami & South Florida. (n.d.). Monkey3. https://www.monkeyjungle.com/